BROKEN MEN

(the cats out of the bag)

JAMES P WILLSHIRE

BALBOA.PRESS

A DIVISION OF HAY HOUSE

Balboa Press books may be ordered through booksellers or by contacting:

Balboa Press
A Division of Hay House
1663 Liberty Drive
Bloomington, IN 47403
www.balboapress.co.uk
UK TFN: 0800 0148647 (Toll Free inside the UK)
UK Local: (02) 0369 56325 (+44 20 3695 6325 from outside the UK)

Print information available on the last page.

ISBN: 978-1-9822-8597-5 (sc)
ISBN: 978-1-9822-8598-2 (e)

Balboa Press rev. date: 06/28/2022

CHAPTER ONE

would like to give some reasons as to why I find it necessary to embark on this piece of work, it is for the saviour of millions of men, brutally beaten down by the state, the church and political correctness, the abuse of men by the above powers has to stop. In my personal opinion and through my personal experiences the need for change is long over due, I wish to make as many people aware of these barbaric and inhumane practices as possible, a little optimistic on my part i here you cry, maybe, but at the very least get to the core of these issues, and the exploitation of power over men into the public arena, and finally have it discussed in a manner and gravity it deserves. If only to protect the small boys who in the future will be subjected to the cynicism inflicted upon them by the very females who supposedly love them, blighted throughout their lives with laws and ideologies alongside skewered indoctrination that are in serious need of recalibration.

I have no formal education in such matters, but have the most important qualification of all, experience, also there is a need for a very outdated resource, common sense, alongside compassion and equality of which these self satisfying, lazy, ruthless beasts who have been elevated to a standing in life beyond belief or understand of why or indeed how they got there.

Being a construction worker, I am ready for the derision, of which will be heaped on me aplenty, i am sure, by the gym going fake tanned narcissists of questionable intellect, and some of the non gym goers with intellect. I am totally unconvinced by all the smoke in the last thirty years which has so emphatically been blown up the arse of these female nonentities, who feel they are the Titans of whatever they choose to take the slightest interest in. I am sure the response of the deluded males across the country, these empty vessels of humanity will no doubt accuse me of sexism, misogyny and portray me as a man whose life has passed him by at the behest of women, all of this may or may not be true, so read on and make your own mind up. If it is not an open one and you are at best feeling a little annoyed, I am sure you will take great pleasure in ripping out the pages as the credits from loose women go up, having dispatched a cheap bottle of sparkling white wine.

If any one is offended by these opening words please read on there is plenty more. If you are easily displeased by anything you do not ascribe to, I hope this is up there with the best. I must state I am not alluding to the fact that all women are the same, but if any of this is wrong you can pick fault, but those who shout loudest will almost certainly have found a section in this work that directly applies to them, all I can say is gotcha.

Undeniably, records in ancient and modern history show in graphic detail the consequences of the actions of misplaced laws and beliefs that directly benefit women, I am trying to describe within these pages the number of fortunes of wealth and property stolen by the way of unbridled deceit alongside biased laws has played a huge part in the denigration of men, the incalculable effect upon these innocent broken men callously deceived, looted and abandoned, to whom the only remedy is taking ones own life or being unable to resist murdering the perpetrator, in this desperate situation the mental deterioration is compounded again and again by wanton bias and pressure from the state the law and the complete lack of either compassion or sense. These men have been corralled into an unhinged degree of financial and emotional violence that in any other walk of life would be outlawed, and with open mouths society would be aghast that this was ever allowed to manifest in the first place. All of these circumstances of unbearable torture and enforced destitution and custody battles along with in most cases the flagrant use of the weapon of mass destruction, also known as the cunt. When at the same time trying to comprehend these matters, and being told constantly "man up", and behave in a restrained, sensible manner throughout, commendable, I am sure, but what of the women.

If a complaint of domestic violence to the police is made, depending on the gender of the complainer the out come will be very different, in my direct experience the answer to a complaint was "we (the police) do not get involved in domestic incidents", on being assaulted with a bottle on my own doorstep by a female, I then informed the police that I would resolve the matter myself, on hearing this response the tone changed and they arrived with in ten minutes. On arrival I was questioned on how much I had to drink, the afore mentioned woman then proceeded to attack the officer, she was handcuffed and arrested. It goes with out saying the next day she was released, no charge. Let's reverse this, if I had attacked a women, on her own doorstep with a bottle would the out come have been the same, if you have to consider this for more than half a second intelligence is most certainly not on your side.

In divorce, the rank inequality is at play in all but a few cases, so why do we marry, habit and conformity and pressure from the female matriarchy, the church also, in the bible it says "then the lord god said it is not good men should be alone. I will make a helper fit for him" (genesis 2:18-25) this in turn set out the early format of pre-marriage, and in Malachi (2:14-15) "to whom you have been faithless, though she is your companion and your wife by covenant" . Covenant meaning concordat or stipulation, this in turn makes it clear that all responsibility, financial and everything else, falls heavily on the man, all of which remains to this day, so although equality is supposed to be the theme of the day, talked about to even the cows wont come home, equality law is for women only, as clearly the modern mind set of law and rights exercised over men is obvious. In the event of a collapsed marriage, the cause is never questioned, men always come off worst, emotionally and of course financially, why they are adhering to a 2000 year old scripture that men should shoulder all responsibility is in need of change. The immeasurable damage done by maintaining these ideologies is long lasting and in many cases irreversible, the thought of a victorian woman poor and defenceless huddled in the dark and damp corner of the scullery with her starving unwashed brood is not evident in these times. Now it goes like this, the man is responsible for keeping them all in a way they are accustomed, 55 inch tv ("we must be entitled to the 70 inch curved m'lud) and just two I pads between three is outrageous depravation, cry the feminists and law upholders.

Marriage is supposed to be the defining moment of adulthood, and in many ways it is, those immortal words "for better or worse" sum up the severe gravity of this under taking, which by the way, is a female led juggernaut of self-serving, over inflated egotists with pompous notions along with the extreme desire to burn money, this trait will continue throughout the partnership.

Then there is the meeting of the parents, to see if you are fit for purpose, the nerve racking venerable meal, to see if you know how to use a knife and fork correctly, so the burden of the daughter can be shifted with out any fear or conscience of a financial disaster, the question of the suiters ability to earn and indeed have substantial monies available, this unsavoury attitude exists wether the parents are wealthy or poor. These financial improprieties will be a constant in all but a few marriages, joint bank accounts where where extremely uncommon until the women entered the workplace, depositing there two hundred pound salary in, and the husband depositing his five hundred pounds. Suddenly in a world of mind bending irrationality the women felt after all the money was lumped together, they became financial equals, thus they had access to all the funds. In the rare event of the wife being the higher earner before any rules are set, there will be an endless set of hoops to jump through to even get near her money. If the man was to conduct himself in this manner the whole scenario would be twisted into some form of oppression "if you loved me, you would trust me" and "i married for love not money" all of which time and time again has been proven a blatant lie.

On entering the vow of marriage which describes itself as solemn, after walking through the apt graveyard, with its manicured lawns, and evergreen bushes which the wife will incidentally become the same shape as. Then into the old building, with its musty smell, where lie after lie has been spewed out over willing victims, to paralyse thought and in still terror that if you deviate from this path, the non-compliance will put them in to cauldron of pain and misery.

It is beyond curious that neither the man or the women ever frequent this building other than to get married, this smacks of hypocrisy from all sides of the need to start their new life in this way.

It is mainly the women who want the church wedding "the big day". It has to be an event of preposterous cost and formalities that will never be encountered again. She wants to look like those coffee table magazine brides, these ridiculously over engineered garments which went out with cinderella and Sid James in the scarlet pimpernel, these period fashion pieces are the very thing women have become, over priced over the top and impractical, the ability to cook, launder (with the machine not down the wash brook)and look after the kids seems to be a requirement brushed under the carpet, where of course when located by the man will be dutifully removed.

Why white, a sign of virginal innocence, another ploy of the church to stop sex before marriage, after all in times gone by the only charity was the church, and they did not want to waste their money on these urchins. Why has this obsession about the dress become so uncanny, in a way that defies all sense and reasoning, it has to be white to portray the wearer as clean and untouched, untainted by life and men. Forget the previous twenty or so dalliances and in many cases the last taste of freedom on the hen party. The very idea of virtuousness is laughable, still the veneer is ensconced in this minefield of untruths, and ambitions with which these predators over a period of time with the investment of the flesh they will reap untold financial benefits, of which otherwise would never have been obtained. When the "i do's" have been exchanged, and the vows inevitably tweaked to her liking, so no offence to her loyal ground breaking followers are in any way made to feel uncomfortable. Now the old building can be vacated, with harrowing sound of the organ behind them to be resurrected another day. This cold and unwelcoming building, of which most of the participants will never enter again, until in a box.

In what seems an eternity inside, the light out side is a welcome reminder all is not lost, laughter reignites the day, confetti is thrown and a much wanted cigarette is lit. Then the ridiculously priced photographs begin, as with the flowers, only the top package will do, the flowers will die and the photographs fade, nevertheless, on her insistence this money is in budget and must be spent, not unlike the foreign aid policies of the UK.

The over enthusiastic photographer then comes into his own, corralling the family and guest into an unimaginable set of sequences, that takes for ever, to make this set of photographs the most original portfolio in history, which of course they are not, they are just another set of images heading for the middle draw of an Ikea special. Maybe resurrected once a year, for the first three, then resigned to posterity.

Then the elaborate proceedings begin, known as the reception, this also means acceptance of all that will occur in this gathering. First up the speeches, all mandatory, yes man der tory, nervous croaky voices of inexperienced orators, the best man does his best to bring to life some amusing historical events, followed by the father of the bride, an intense gloss over of the daughter beyond belief, then it's the turn of the groom, usually a diatribe of cringing arse licking to all and sundry, and of course the new wife will worshipped at every chance, a manner she will expect from there on in. Alongside the pledge of financial and emotional impunity to be hers, obedience must displayed in public at all times, and a proclivity for the man to weep uncontrollably in circumstances she feels are warranted, or the lack of empathy and compassion will be deeply in question. Throughout all the proceedings sits there soaking up the unearned adoration of individuals, some she has never met, but are required to engage in this circus, the mantras of "you look beautiful" etc etc, the bar is know set for all happenings in the future, and the husband will be constantly reminded of the content of this day. She doesn't even stand, why is this, women also are not great orators (only behind closed doors), so again the women are spared yet another uncomfortable situation due to gender, yet all the other tawdry extravaganza is firmly under their control. The ridiculous attempt to reenact some magazine pull out, on a tenth of the budget, is tacky and ludicrous, justified by "this is the biggest day of her life" (not his ?), this is the self-entered attitude that will be present at all times throughout her life, and in many cases this will incur huge and avoidable debt. This in turn will in many instances suffocate the marriage, which swirls around in a financial morass, how will this pan out, she usually emerges unscathed, due to help from male family members, misguided by the indoctrination of the state that it is the man duty to do so. So how does the man fair in all this, not good, with perpetual interference by the state, homeless and pursued with financial restraints on him, to adhere to biased outdated laws, the will lead to poverty and mental health issues, all this whilst she is cocooned in belief by all she is more vital than him.

CHAPTER TWO

We must break free from the antiquated way in which we portray men, after all the constant reinvention of women to bolster up their worth is an unstoppable non-science of grotesque untruths. The reason to push women to the front of all things, no matter how much bias or inequality is needed, is deemed necessary to avoid the destruction of mankind, by eager button pushing male despots, of whom are totally out of control, and in desperate need of the feminine touch to avoid the inevitable. The great new minds, who wish to distort and address all the short comings of men, from parenting to mowing the lawn are in an ascendancy of bewildering pace, this onslaught is justified by the need for equality, this blanket reasoning is an implausible argument. The need for everything to be equal, because that's only fair, is in it's self a some what simplistic vision an unprofessional, idiotic notion, that only the uneducated and the hell bent extremist would pertain to.

Equal in what is my question, is it in everything, or just what the women wants to be involved in, or what is best for them, and what suits them, or what they are comfortable doing, the list is endless even before the myth of equality is employed by the law and state. The glaringly obvious reason behind all huffing and puffing is women want equality in every thing they want, and not in anything they don't, because in equality expectations become higher, for example in the work place, more hours, more commitment, these things may well be unreachable, due to many things.

The main one being, we are different, or maybe that's a contentious issue too.

Over time the relationships and cohabitations of men and women and children has worked, it has been the norm for centuries, not to mention times of poverty and extreme hardship was an everyday occurrence, a myriad of problems had to overcome just to survive, by and large men and women did this together, so this suggests in the past this was a successful format.

Over the last half century there has been an explosion of new laws and regulations, with angst and bitterness whipped up in to a frenzy for the need for equality at all cost. All of these demands to enhance the female agenda with or with out proper reasoning is damaging and blind, the endless complaining of inequality has meant the subjection of men to female demands and wishes, this has constructed an uneven playing field, to which the male has to forfeit not only emotional pain, financial rape, and indeed slaughter of his dignity, while his young children look on oblivious to the dismantlement of their own father, conducted with consent by the law and the state onlooking.

Even in the social arena men are treated in an unequal manner, in a pub I noticed two signs "MEN, no shirt, no shoes, no service " this was on the entrance, a threat before the man even entered, this type of coercion is rarely aimed at women, once inside there was above the bar another sign "WOMEN, no skirt, free drinks". Now who is being marginalised here, the man is told non-compliance and the venue is out of bounds and the woman if dressed in a provocative manner will receive complimentary drinks. The very thought of bare chested men marauding spiralling out of control and god forbid barefooted in a holiday resort, not to mention spending 80% of all the cash in the till. This type of inequality is also prevalent in the night club sphere, the dress codes always aimed at men, the stipulation the man must wear shoes, not trainers, a collared shirt, trousers not jeans, once all the hoops have been successfully negotiated, they will be permitted to pay and enter this so called public facility. What of the female patron, as long as she can stand she's in, and sometimes when propped up entrance is not a problem. With leopard print see through dresses no underwear is a sight any red blooded male can endure hour after hour, the only distraction is a better equipped one, this charade is all for the procurement of free entrance and free drinks, an extremely successful ploy, but not one to admit, due to the thought of dressing to please the men in order to get what they want.

Then when the clock strikes twelve a change occurs, all be it slowly, but it is noticeable all the same, after the early drinks are consumed during the ritual of making ones self fit for public viewing (many times this act is a gravely comical failure) the alcohol begins to subvert these beautiful creatures. On starting the night out with little money on board, they seek any venue with bias rules, that favour women over men, "ladies free night" for example, I have yet to come across "men go free night". Drinks come thick and fast from well known soft touches (a little wink suggesting maybe his luck is in tonight), and also complete strangers, in what other walk of life would any one except a free anything from an unknown person, never mind an alcoholic drink in the dark, were conversation is limited at best. Once the sufficient point is reached, any thing can happen, a mis-placed word or hand can light the fuse, all of the over-reaction will noticed, cries of "leave her alone" accompanied by much high pitched screaming, than the man may well be doused in the very liquid her not five minutes ago purchased, and was received in good humour.

Then the doyen of the rabble comes to the rescue, usually fat, tattooed and with many children, the bulk is an intimidating sight, bingo wings flapping, rings on every finger (total value under fifty quid), with thighs like seals waists, demanding an apology, "and don't forget that drink you made waste". Then the doorman get's involved, his mind set is if I deal with this situation I may well have a chance of getting in a pair of knickers, the male is thrown out after the much fluttering of eyelashes. The male turning on another due to the belief he will receive sexual gratuities is just another divisive act that women can so easily employ, unless you are extremely handsome, like Ted Bundy for example, the shallow mind of a woman is hard to enter, and we all known the outcome this scenario.

The Welsh government in 2019 caved into female demands to wear trousers in a manner beyond any thing other than a pathetic joke, to justify the allowing girls to wear trousers they gender neutralised the school uniform, this in turn meant boys can wear skirts. Is this freedom of choice or just another give away to women, any idiot knows the boys will not wear skirts. In the pure folly of this one of the reasons given for change was "global warming", if so to hotter summers why would girls want to wear trousers, once the law was passed (because much of the time it's the act of forcing change, that's the driver) many wore skirts anyway. This is just petty interference by those who can, in order to devour anything in pink. Back to the "no skirt free drinks", imagine a man with his cock and bollocks bulging out in pair tighty whities, this sounds like a looming arrest to me, why you may ask, the answer is because most complainers are women.

Wimbledon tennis tournament is a shining example of equal pay for less work, less ability, less crowd attraction, all these things women are guilty of, yet equal pay was announced as if it was a ground breaking act of human enhancing magnitude that was necessary, the reason I suggest in a simplistic way possible is because they are playing the same game. There is rather a large elephant on court, although of course not visible a certain amount of sniggering is definitely audible, but still the commentators are silent, and any one who wants to remain on yet another establishment gravy train remain immune to any question of equal pay for equal work solely because in this instance the huge benefit to women. The women semi-final and final combined less than two hours, just the men's final over five hours. Five hours work versus one hours work, same pay because you are a woman, if only I could find such a job in my favour, any business owner would throw this format out as pure fantasy, and rightly so. Wimbledon's justification of this nonsense is that men and women spend the same amount of time on preparation, this is as lame a donkey on daytime television, the truth is many people devout there whole lives to one sport or another, they never reach the top, should they be paid also?. The entrance fee is the same price for one hours entertainment as five hours, no matter how you dress it up or down the comparison is deeply flawed, from start to finish this equality is presided over by unshaven women and weeping men, in a kangaroo court terrified of not securing the next lucrative contract for their inclusion and the salaries that go with it, they drive home their views and woes of female sports being underfunded, mis-understood and under represented in the media. The nuts and bolts of it are simple, if no body watches it, no body sponsors it, no matter how many ways bias for women's sport is employed the truth of the matter is in male dominated sports women will never but much good, never mind great. These male sports undertaken by women are fine, but they will never be as watchable as the men, the cry of underfunding is a sexist crime, when will they understand, hardly anyone is interested, let alone will go and pay to watch it. In rugby being fat is the main requirement for women, and the ability to drink pints of piss and eat shit sandwiches, this can only be to emulate their male peers, this is just another example of how low woman will go to be in a man's world, and invade his space in the childish notion of " why can't I do that", no matter how distasteful it may be. Most of these forays into male sports are spectacular failures, with mis-appropriated funds to the detriment of young boys, who have genuine talent, that is the only crime here in sporting terms, pure disregard for promising young boys for the sake of equality, that due to natural physicality the boy has a better chance of success. Where physicality is not an issue, darts or snooker say, then shows men have more mental toughness, work ethic in practice and will to win, this difference is mainly due to the woman's benefitting of the rub of the green or pink shall we say from day one, by male family members, much will and determination has long since waned by a female reaching adolescence.

Back to Wimbledon, if woman is top of the tree in her field, which is the second tier, men are top of the first tier, this makes the woman less competent than the men, so why equal pay?, only until it is a totally integrated tournament, winner takes all, can equal pay by be in any way plausible. Or maybe the male competition one week female the next, this will never happen, the lack of crowds would be to evident, and sponsorship would drop on the second week, imagine winner takes, there never be another woman's name scratched on that trophy again, quality talent and prowess swept aside by the despicable term inequality, women are like children asking for ice-cream, once the parent is so fed up of hearing this they give in, mines a 69.

The men seem to be involved in the housework more and more, this is a stab at equality in the household, and no doubt a sense of misguided fairness to all the overworked, undervalued and obscenely underpaid women, in part-time, menial jobs, who feel so hard done by the lot they have drawn in life. With the carpet hoovered, by the hoover he paid for, in the act of servility, "to in some small way to balance up the ridiculous and divisive term "unpaid work", which is becoming a blight and sad reality of modern times. Pilates at nine on a Sunday morning, a ploy to escape the drudgery of getting the kids up and fed, after all it's his only day off, so "it' your turn with the kids, it's alright for you, you have been at work all week", and off she goes, in lycra with a small pink mat and unwashed ponytailed hair. On returning, showered and reinvigorated, she looks at her husband, unshaven, tired in grey joggers, and thinks there must be more to life then this. She then embarks to a world of fantasy aided by the likes of Hello and You magazines, with grinding articles spelling out her own dilemma to the point of perfection, alongside a few more pitfalls for future use. The realisation they are not alone in this brutal world of inequality and entrapment, must be extremely comforting, and extremely counter productive, with the abuse of their human rights, which is holding them back, not allowing them to reach the very pinnacle they feel was their god given destiny, regardless of effort or competence, the cries to remove this heavy chain from around woman kinds neck across the world.

This illusion is what women try to create around themselves in this pantomime rehearsal played out behind hundreds of thousands of front doors far and wide, of which brow beaten families have to adhere to, in order to placate these ungrateful selfish beasts. Women are constantly reminded and convinced, they should be in a better place than the one they are in, indoctrination tells them this is so, with out determination or effort the prize should be forthcoming due to their gender, just be the act of dropping their knickers (a sad fact is this is all most women have to bargain with).

When the plan fails miserably, some one has to pay, and we all know who that is, the man has to to be defiled, to the detriment of his children by the state and the selfish ideology of the mother.

We are blindly heading into a part of world order that in history will be called out as one of the the most damaging and backward eras of all time. The inclusion of all people in all matters, no matter what level of intellect or competence, in the name of diversity, "the need to include", this rhetoric is playing right into the manicured hands of the feminists, as long as inclusion to they parts of this hard life they don't want are not included, hard manual work and taking the dog for an early morning walk in the winter, to mention just two. To many old white men in the hierarchy, these men of experience and rationale must be expunged and wiped of the face of the earth, in order to make way for free thinking women, who have compassion, this with no experience is a catastrophe, a recipe to undermine all things that benefit and help society function. Woe betide any one who disagrees, man or woman, to let these female crusaders any where near power or governance and expect them to show impartiality is laughable and stupid. With the relatively new "women only shortlist" another set problems arise, enamouring the unsuitable over the suitable due to gender will help no one, not even the women who are hell bent that this is the way to go.

With senseless mind bending pig headedness, should be a warning, this war all that is not fair or what women deem as unfair, is becoming a parody that no one dare call out, due to the brevity of discussion that is allowed to take place, the attack on any thing male is taken as just, the ridiculous and damaging notion that by including women will improve any scenario you care to mention is for the birds. The calamitous thought police are doing all in their illegal and unelected positions to enforce the ideology in homes, school and the workplace to give women the upper hand in all sectors which will confiscate any equalities that now exist, solely because the women think it's their turn.

Whenever a subject is freely discussed between men and woman the excuse is that men are afraid of women, to allow women into all areas due to the fear of being surpassed, this fear is dramatically over used as to show men are weak and unable to defend the things that they excel in, men are dominant in areas due to competence and suitability, not just because they are men, it is preposterous to suggest any other reason. With the ever growing bias and discrimination against men shown by the government bodies who are willing to twist and turn in any direction to flout any sensible outcome, with machinations fully supported by the ever increasing involvement of the state, is the male chagrin along with the blind dead end ally it is hurtling into. Pompous prevarication on a monumental scale is happening in all arenas, in the name of equality, a flawed and dangerous ideology, solely for the benefit of women, this is causing irreversible damage to society on mass. When questions arise concerning this meteoric unchecked rise of women above all men in all things, the playground insults begin behind the the workplace computer screens (in between online shopping and booking nail and hair appointments) the catcalls of mummies boy is frightened of women.

With all this new found power and alleged insight women are said to posses in abundance, alongside the Darlek like mantra "diversify, diversify", has any of this made any difference, are houses any cheaper, are the starving any less hungry, has the world dropped a couple of degrees, do bears no longer shit in the woods, a loud and resounding "no" is the answer. Is there a baby changing shelf in train toilets, maybe, is there a breast feeding station in Macdonalds, maybe, is there more opportunities in the construction industry (manual work not included) not taken up certainly, are there more useless university courses, yes, are there more women only shortlists, yes, with all this innovation forced and drilled into anything that is deemed to be in range, has much changed, no. The glass ceiling alongside the glass table have been shat on and paid with nothing other than female gain in mind, and ultimately there has been little or no return.

As for the mealy mouthed men with no agenda of their own, and hang on every mono- syllabic word with a gaping jaw, the act of not thinking for themselves is being enforced by controlling women intent on dictating every step of the way, or else. These empty shells are becoming useless and worthless in the name of equality, unable to make a phone call about a defective product, choose a babies name or where they are to be married, all these choices have been smuggled away in the name of progress. When one sits in a cafe at the local garden centre or else where, the cringing statement "me and ma missus", from a man who has never been food shopping alone, never holidayed alone, and never gone to bed on his own for the last thirty years, the decline of men has never been more evident due to the false empowerment of women.

What have these once proud, outgoing funny men become, disintegrated into shallow, two dimensional beings with no spontaneity in life, all the deviances from the other halves programme or preferences is seen as wilful disobedience and a serious danger to the status quo, she has over many years so skilfully put into place, with out him even being aware. Only from the outside and only by men who have escaped this control and not got back into the control, can feel so what's really going on. A deft deployment of unwritten rules and regulations (as i-phone to i-pad) in such a subtle manner, that has been constructed carefully alongside rafts of new regulations by the state and any other body that feels the discrimination of men, the oppression of men is necessary and and indeed morally just. The slow lobotomising of ones loved one? Is akin to manslaughter, the slow death of inner feeling and thought, the breaking of will to be ones self and to take part in the game of life, has been eroded away in the name of equality. This is evident at the local supermarket during "the weekly shop", where he shuffles behind the trolly and she barks out what is to be placed within, sometimes she even asks him of his preference to a certain item, which has already been dispatched and heading for the over-filled trolly, a morass of products that tells you all you need to know about them. These men are lost soles wandering in the park in the cold winter days, told to leave while she does the housework, the newly retired man after fifty years of work is now surplus to requirements, a sad truth of society that only recognises ones value whilst paying tax, the interest in the retired man is of grinding decline, his reason for being, his career over, then there's her, unforgiving due to the feeling that the freedom she has enjoyed for decades is up, and it's his fault for having the audacity to retire after fifty years at work.

After a while the retired man begins to join in with the house work, at least he doesn't need to be out any more, enduring the more taxing of duties is a small price to pay. The reward for all these years loyalty and obsequiousness the man is met with contempt and derision, finishing his sentences and making him a fool in front of others with great delight, this form of control may seem harmless, but it is deeply embedded in the female psyche to get her own back, after centuries of the feeling of being overlooked and down trodden by men. This self induced state of all consuming hatred of men is rarely admitted or shown for that matter in public, she can ill afford to upset his family or friends and any children they may have, the woman is very careful to conceal her true thoughts (only in an all female group can she come clean) feelings and actions, this is all part of the deceptive manner in which she will conduct her self through out her life. If her true colours where to be shown all credence of the charade she plays of the one being controlled would be lost, the charade is easy to play due to the physical size of men which suggests they are the ones in control. This is the smoke screen women operate under with aplomb. The very slightest undermining of a female by a male, wether it be a conversational contradiction or a derisory comment on clothing is seen as a violent onslaught to her dignity and wellbeing, these matters are blown up out of all proportion, so that in any male criticism no matter how insignificant can be whipped up into an attack of a most dastardly kind which must be silenced at all costs, for the saviour of all women across the world, to end this bullying that has existed since dinosaurs roamed the earth, when mister Pterodactyl became a little annoyed over missus Pterodactyl non-compliance and let out one roar over the ones which would have been deemed as satisfactory.

Amending bills to enable positive discrimination in the female favour as the Labour Party did in 2002, in favour of female only MPs to stand in certain seats, which most where safe seats and even then some where lost, this shows there is no way integrity and honour can be forced.

Now in 2020 the labour party has imploded like no other party in the history of politics, so how has this gender based doctrine helped. It is obvious this has been a divisive force that in no way can it be said is good for any free thinking country. Yet still this falsehood remains, " women first" continues, with the notion women must be given their chance to lead, women have no shame or reason to demand this other than that they are women, this self delusion, regardless of suitability or competence, shows a complete lack of intelligence and understanding, with a blind belief that suggests any thing other than motherhood, can be socially engineered successfully in the females favour and gender is the only defining factor.

It seems to me there is a insatiable desire, by women to get their noses in the trough and once this is accomplished followed by a sideways glance that says we did it, once the bloated salaries and the gold plated pensions obtained, political empathy only in name remains. At the end of the day, if you spend too much of some one else"s money, (which for most women is standard), without the correct results, the remaining in any position is precarious, then we are back to the cry of sexism, so a full circle has been drawn. So the male form of fiscal matters and common sense is upheld due to the fact it was the better model from the very start. With historical proof of decades of experience without interference, to draw upon, it remains, women at all costs avoid any acknowledgement of this, of which is there for all to see, in the main guys got it right.

We need change, why, because women said so, that's not an argument any sane person could uphold, so when, the state has bulldozed laws and acts to one side, to facilitate the female superiority, in an unfair, undemocratic manner, that the world should be ashamed, this gender cleansing will in the future be seen as a travesty, just to fulfil the narcissism these women posses in abundance, and when they fail which they are and will continue to do so, when no men have been involved, thus no blame can be applied to men, they will then blame each other. This totally avoidable train wreck will serve no purpose at all, let's just hope the damage will be recognised soon and be repairable.

The empowerment of women, this is another inequality to enhance the female, to of course will be detrimental to the man. Just another way to put women first, a discriminating tool, backed by rafts of written laws (along with unwritten ones) and screeching women, to make sure the first bite of the apple is theirs, then and only then they will decide if the apple is for them or not. As to wether the apple is to sweet, sour, crisp or soft, if not to the woman's liking it can be passed to the male, reluctantly of course. The empowerment mantra is said to have for core elements, Information, inclusion/participation, accountability and local organisation capacity.

Information is there for young or old, male or female. What type of special information do men have that women do not, as usual the smoke screen and mirrors theory applies, this is in order for the advance of women, regardless of suitability or competence, into places, where they would not have reached, jobs or positions they are not capable of carrying out. You would not give just anyone a trowel to build a house, but as in the many instances of the work women choose, unlike the unqualified bricklayer, who's lack of competence will be evident in a very short period of time, due to shoddy look of the brick work, they women are under reams of paperwork and guidelines, behind phone calls and group meetings, so their level of incompetence slips quietly under the radar, until it is to late, once found out the pay off is made and all is hushed up.

Inclusion/participation, this sounds like something straight out of the primary school class room, which should not surprise any one, as this sector is nearly exclusively by women foe women. To include, also needs the ones (women) to wish to be included, this, as in all engineered bias to the female is deeply flawed. As the cherry picking of careers, political positions etc, the balance is lost to the easier options, and indeed opt out at will, through no fault of their own, other than a loss of interest or the going got tough. All of these fake quangos at huge tax payers cost for the inclusion of women, in what ever they fancy, goes to prove, if the individual is not interested they will definitely not participate, no matter how much spin is applied.

Accountability is a form of behaviour that females learn to avoid at a very early age. Childhood bestows upon the young girls the feeling of worth, that will be female agenda through out their lives, this is never so of boys, it would be unspeakable to instruct sexism in boys, yet this is prevalent in the up bringing of girls, with the belittlement of boys and derision of dads that takes place in most domestic situations. But within all this flattery and self-appointment of the females, by the females, the golden rule is in any drama or disaster it's not the woman's fault, it's a man's world?, thus they are accountable, not us poor little women. This unaccountability is evident in many simple tasks, and that is the myth we are expected believe blown out of the water (as long as the man installs the dynamite), with the event of a puncture, man and woman in the car, who will step up and be accountable, physical strength may be an issue, but not as big an issue as competence to carry out the change and maybe encounter a little muck. So as in many situations at an early age the woman is conditioned to be unaccountable and the man is responsible for any distasteful elements that life may throw at them, and don't let him forget to pay the bill at the same time, this is a life long trait installed in women, if the man fails the state will dutifully step up.

Local organisation capacity, what an earth does that mean. Does it imply the amount of cash which can be thrown at the deluded idea of the empowerment of women, until the men are battered into submission by fake figures and desires for women fully met, councils agendas forced into towing the line by political correctness, positive discrimination taught in night-school courses, to take the female intelligence to a level unheard of (still is). When this level of super intelligence is reached, will she observe the social engineering involved, and feel a little embarrassed by the imbalance of gender opportunity that has been afforded to them, no is the answer, as these women lay waste to a humility, that will without doubt be a big problem for society in the future.

We are led to believe that empowerment for women needs to be carefully nurtured and plenty of leeway must be applied, so we do not frighten these delicate beings away from their righteous path to achievement, success and wealth, so even when it appears women are not quite hitting they mark, they must be convinced they are. We are to listen to women with full attention as not to marginalise them, inducing insecurity, why are they insecure, when one is out of ones depth, this is a natural reaction. Believe in women, should we not believe in all.

Forgive women's mistakes in their new found equality as not to alienate them and in some way perturb them from fulfilling the pinnacle of which they were destined to reach. Surly the only way to deal with a mistake is to confront it and deal with it, no matter who is at fault, the carpet should never be raised and the broom applied.

The issue of feelings is a female trait to overcome many responsibilities throughout all walks of life, it is bad enough walking on eggshells at home, because of a self imposed sensitivity, so why would this behaviour be tolerated in the workplace. This is another divisive tool used by women to distance themselves from the obvious inadequacies they possess. This emotional, freely displayed weakness employed to great effect is another reason why the difference in men and women will never close, men grow potatoes and women used to cook them, now unless a substantial benefit is to be acquired, the special meal comes from the newly liberated male in belief he is more women than she is, soon the boxed meals and the ping of the microwave is the norm, him, as the relationship develops to busy at work, her to busy in forging the life of being kept women, minimal work, washed and peeled produce delivered at his expense. This propensity to emotional disablement of women is another falsehood to enable women to get what they want, playing on the damsel in distress has long been a format women rely on, when questioned about this, it is denounced, we are stronger than men, live longer, bear children, champion all dangers alone, support our selves, pay their own bills, build their own houses, maintain their own cars, invent many things, are mathematicians, scientists, pioneers of equality and founders of the basic truths and morals of modern society, er no.

As a study revealed in 2013, over thirteen million women were classed as employed, out of these, 42% were part-time, thus subsidised by their male partners or the state. These figures have been maintained forth best part of thirty years. So with all the empowerment, all women short lists, decades of discrimination against the bed rock of the workforce, namely men, what has been achieved, very little. This smacks into the face of this mantra of female empowerment, most women just don't want it, the more skilled the job is, the harder it is to perform, the more accountability and responsibility, women just don't want it, women in general don't want to work under the pressure these conditions demand and many simply could not. Women will, and always have chosen the easy option in the workplace, so let's not get carried away with the notion that equality at work, is the single most important cornerstone to build the whole of society off, there must be many out there who will think for five logical unemotional, non-hormonal, unbiased minutes, that this has been nothing other than a crusade for those fashionable gender equality partisan agency, equality solutions, the empowerment of wimmins league, and any other diabolical set of numpties you care to mention, of which there are many, alongside the radical female nobodies who can think of nothing original, so after more than century has passed, reenact the chaining of women to the nearest government owned railings, as if laughably, conditions were in any way comparable in 2020. All of these actions and government financed bodies are in full cry for some thing women do not want, equality. Equality is not to be taken when it suits, it is to be in place at all times in all areas and situations, it cannot be cherrypicked, if cherrypicking is aloud, this will undermine any credibility that has been gained, a misrepresentation of equality entirely. It is all very commendable to demand the right to have an equal chance to do any job they want, but is extremely disappointing that behind all the millions of pounds of tax payers money on campaigns, this rhetoric is empty and a blatant cop out.

This marching around London by desperate women and the fools that accompany them is preposterous in it's spectacle and without any solid validity, this non-stop parading of bewildered three year olds which in some way these women think will ad a little sympathy to plight they are having to endure is utter nonsense, and all of this whilst the husband is at work, funding the train tickets and Macdonalds children meals to cap a wonderful productive day out, because sadly that's all it is. This behaviour is dishonest and extremely distasteful, the shameful mantras these women espouse, shows the freedom they have, the time on their hands, to do things most of us would never contemplate, let alone have time to do.

These fake ideologies are not only damaging to the very cause women behold, but show how selfish and deluded these angst riddled hypocrites are way of the mark in knowing exactly what they are demanding. This in it's self shows an overhaul of common sense needs to be applied. At no time will women feel they have come a long way, until they capsize the boat of which they have been rocking, this will be to the detriment of all.

Whilst the state and any other think tank or organisation, publicly funded of course, these idealists are not worth their salt, never mind any other mineral known to man, continue in this failed witch hunt giving false hopes, to false people, who are in it for an easy ride, cloaked in the guise of political correctness and gender equality, grow up and develop some intuition and stop following a path littered with obstacles of their own making, nothing will be achieved in an honest and sensible fashion. The ambivalence of all they represent is clear, so is the damage it causes, as does any law or policy enforced upon a free thinking society. We of whom have the slightest interest in history will be aware of certain regimes in the past who have steam rolled their populations into submission, in the name biased treatment to the unworthy, this does not work out well. These actions will cause in the future, out rage and public discourse, as it has always done. In China for example, any public suppression can be maintained by force, media control and many other measures not in play in the western world. So the folly of these divisive doctrines imposed on already egalitarian societies will be uncovered as the fraud it has become.

As in all these de facto wars waged for the equality of the down trodden element of society, (women) can only damage any belief in it's reasoning or the gaining of support, due to the fact that the very people they rally around to snatch from the jaws of imminent poverty and slaughter, are in fact are doing very well and have not been instructed never mind consulted as to the danger, to which they may succumb. This is a trait widely employed be all those who know best for all people, in all things, at all costs, which are usually higher than the status quo.

CHAPTER THREE

n the workplace a myth has been installed that men and women are equal, this is another way of putting women first, no matter how unsuitable or competent they are. Take the physical aspect, a sheer imbalance in strength exists between men and women, yes I am sure there are many women stronger than some men, and I am sure many quotes and personnel recollections, to bare this out can be plucked from memory (these memories are so memorable, due to the fact of their scarcity) but being realistic one must admit in general men are stronger than women, if you are a little unsure in this, simply check all the current weightlifting records for a little clarity. Physical strength comes into play in countless ways in the ability to do the job in front of you. The construction industry for example, in the construction of roads, the lifting of 60 kilo kerbstones, yes there are mechanical ways to lift them, of which any serious kerb layer will tell you are far to slow to make any money, when on piece-work. In paving the handling of 65 kilo precast concrete slabs is required (no mechanical way to lay those), until all these materials are made of foam and can be installed in a warm dry climate the participation of women will be non-existent. some women may paint, or even lay, the odd brick, but as in all things the easy path will be scuttled along in true female fashion, to the sales office, or sectorial role in the warm and dry, or air conditioning they require to function.

If anyone out there feels that the very nature of male dominance in any one particular work place is putting women off, I find this incorrect and inexcusable, it's the nature of the workplace and the work required within it, these are the factors why women omit themselves from these jobs. I can enlighten you all about a failed project, to get more women into the construction industry, an all female construction college, sexist I know, but the desperation to address this issue (why) felt the need to spend a vast amount of money on again some thing woman do not want to be part of.

This earth shattering plan was to avoid intimidation, wolf whistling, and exposure to the odd hairy arse crack to name but a few, with all this careful thought, and social engineering, the enrolment figures rose to a mighty four, hence the college was then opened to males, this inclusion of the very gender which will actually work in construction was the only way to make the college viable.

The nuts and bolts of it are, they were not comfortable with the early starts, and the travelling on cold icy places they were not familiar with, out all day in the heat of summer, no holiday money, no sick pay, and a need to hold ones end up regardless. Also with in this detached world of work we now have to endure, imagine the raft of legislation the implementing of positive discrimination, to the detriment of men, untenable quotas, alongside complete disregard for compatibility and a need to posses the ability to carry out the tasks the salary requires. The whole industry would be clogged up with claim after claim, all due to the incessant need to keep hammering the square peg into an already battered round hole.

Then with in any business the special requirements surrounding pregnancy, maternity pay, the training of another to do the now vacated position, maybe this is temporary or maybe not. If the woman returns, the baby will inevitably affect her performance, mentally and physically. The so called baby blues, which I my opinion is nothing other than a decrease in interest of the new baby, the novelty wears a little thin, after all the coo cooing and plethoras of compliments, gifts and unusual full attention of the husband, when all these things wane the stark reality of motherhood hits home, this can turn joy int misery, so I am told. With the need to employ a temporary replacement comes cost, a watertight contract must be in place, this could be one of the factors as to wether a small business would sink or sail, when the new mum wishes to return.

Then after nearly a year out the hankering for part-time, or indeed no time becomes inevitably evident in the performance at work, all of these issues and more, have to be discussed in an over emotional and suffice to say nearly always to the woman's benefit. A few tears and doctor's notes will terrify her employer and force them to avoid any legal action which in many ways, as in to many things rely on the fragility of her emotional state, this card is played over and over again throughout her life, somewhat odd that the very people who champion the notion of female superiority over men allow this to transpire.

Then there is the issue of sexual discrimination, which is almost totally in the woman's favour, with farcical cases being allowed to manifest by the Guardian reading philosophers that feel all men are sexist bigots, who need to be dealt with in a manner that will shock all others into never replicating these heinous acts. As in one famous case of the award winning scientist of the University College of London Sir Tim Hunt, who commented on female staff, " you fall in love with them, they fall in love with you and when you criticise them, they cry", a quote that after the media and the feministas had caught their breathe had a field day with. This kitten killing, family splitting monster, who just so happens to be a Noble Prize winner and Honorary Member has to be sacrificed, the loss of such rare talent is a shameless act by those in control to maintain the endless pursuit of total control.

The work-like banter, a phrase coined by many, is an exchange of words of slightly derogatory meaning, in a jocular fashion, and when the comment usually of physical nature or criticism of ones work, this was taken with mainly an indifferent manner and amusement. That was until the fluffy laws of the Sexual Discrimination Act, were to unfold and blight the work place, this again to mostly protect the fragility of women. This in hand with ambulance chasing lawyers, who once the gravy train hit full steam ahead, no win no fee, a compensation bonanza had arrived, this brought another inequality for men, the very people who pioneered these industries nurtured them for the huge benefit to others, and in some cases died for this dream have to suffer. The very comments which emboldened the workforce now tear it apart (mainly since the inclusion of women) with the connivance of all management levels beaten into "doing the right thing", their fear of disciplinary action because they failed to take action, this is how sensible managers are duped into taking actions on the filmiest of accusations, that otherwise would have been dealt with in a different manner.

The narrative of "unpaid work has become an extremely contentious issue, of course we are led believe it is only women who suffer this curse of modern day slavery, this rhetoric is a mercenary term conjured up by the wining and the greedy, who want all things, at all times, at every one else's cost, other than their own. The term "house wife" has been demeaned and denigrated and absolutely unashamedly tainted as a position of low rank for the underachievers, which is a slur on one of the most important endeavours undertaken in society. It never ceases to amaze how these women can down grade this once enshrined and respected undertaking, and at the same time, elevating themselves in other positions (eg. Politics) where they have not got a clue, and are only there because of biology and to balance up the numbers. That sit around tables with the very people they despise and badmouth, a line of hypocrisy that they are actually feel they have arrived at this stage on merit is pathetic and laughable. How they look down on nature and normality, in their Laura Ashley double drop waist frocks (to hid the dropped waist). Whilst quaffing Prosecco in wine bars across the city after a hugely important day "at the office" they idly face time their children goodnight.

I suppose the question is should house wives be paid, to my mind they already are, she is fed and watered, has place to live and a bed to sleep in, not free in any hotel I know of, she has clothes and usually a car, medical cover (paid for by his taxes), holidays, meals out, the list is endless, add it up and wise up, this is far from "unpaid work", and don't forget the joint bank account, the demise of many a hardworking man.

Cooking is another chore said by women t be "unpaid work", cooking used to be an important pass time, helping mum in the kitchen of the family home, which brought mother and daughter closer and bonded them for a happier future, which is now callously sniped at by microwave mums of the modern era.

Women now moan they have to go out to work to makes ends meet, maybe so, but in most cases it is to shore up the over stretched budget of greed and want. As the women are sucked in like a bit of fluffing the obscene world of on-line shopping and mobile phone bingo, which has become the preserve of facile uninteresting idlers, who now see the housewife as a failure of this cesspool of existence called life. The rates of divorce, child abuse, children turning to crime, and a whole myriad of social upheaval, is in many cases a result of absent mothers. This I due women engaging in unnecessary work, for unnecessary things, in the mis-guided mindset they equal, then the so called have it all mums now complain of heavy workloads and schedules ruining their lives, it's an old saying "be careful what you wish for, you might get it", and now they have it, they don't want it.

Expecting to be paid for an event solely in your control, and 100% avoidable, is like wanting compensation, from who, the husband the state or both, all of this leaves a bad taste in the mouth for many reasons, the thought of expecting payment for bringing another life to the table of humanity, and all the demands that go with it, food, water, education and medical needs, just to name a few is insane.

Why is it women have so many children when they are so aware of all this "unpaid work", which will dramatically increase with each child, any person who would take on more work of their own freewill, fully knowing they will not be paid for would be an idiot. This is where the myth of "unpaid work" begins to unravel, more kids more state benefits, hand out after hand out, free housing, and on the way back from the food bank don't forget the fags, contraception never put food on the table or a roof over ones head. As for cleaning, what's all the fuss about, who wants to live in a shit hole, it should be a natural response, the wish to live in a clean and healthy environment is an overwhelming must, if something is dirty clean it, soon women will want paying to lay in the bath, due to the fact they got sweaty doing the hoovering.

If a cleaner is employed, due to the immeasurable demands of life foisted upon the working mum, cleaning now becomes "paid work". This is because the mess being cleaned is some one else's mess, this goes to show manufacturing children and making a mess is the sole responsibility of whom ever has control over the above situation, this in it's self does not warrant any payment to some one acting freely.

Housework rosters pinned on fridge doors, by fridge magnets of holidays long gone, (what is the hourly rate for suitcase packing, or rubbing suncream on the kids, on the all expenses paid trip) who does what in the home, and when, is another way she can control the family. With times and activities carefully mapped out, to avoid any wasted spare time or shirked responsibility by five year olds, through out the festival of "unpaid work".

With all this "unpaid work" undertaken in marriage, surely a record should be kept, so any outstanding monies can be re-united with the unsuspecting employees. The reason 95% of households have a stay at home mum is because it is the only financially viable option, that is why women carry out most of domestic chores, what else will she do all day, whilst the husband is at work.

The man's "unpaid work" is as in many man v woman issues swept dutifully under the carpet in the name of unfairness, to which women must always be in the spotlight of any lack of understanding doing the rounds, just in case the lose the drop in "the blame game", with the mantra that men are prioritised, overpaid, underworked beasts in a world that must be overhauled in the name of humanity and equal opportunity, that must not be derailed at any cost, even the introduction of sense and reason must be brushed away with a firm swipe of the marigold. The growing of fresh vegetables in allotments tucked away in cities is the preserve mainly of men some retired, some not, (we can all name, I suspect, a token female allotment owner), this sometimes harsh environment, weather wise, is another place women do not want to be, the men would ridicule the very idea they should be paid for a pastime loved by so many. Then the maintenance on the family car, many bruised and bloodied knuckles sustained (almost all male), in an attempt to keep the vehicle road worthy, in a financially challenging time, all knowledge gained on a learn as you go basis, a trait hardly ever found in the female, due to a lack of will to take on a challenge which is her sole responsibility of the outcome. If he did not succeed in the task not only him getting to work was in jeopardy, thus no money coming in, also shopping trips and days out would be sorely missed, not to mention the odd rush to A-E with the kids.

It is a common site (go look) in DIY stores across the land to see women prodding their men and pointing at shelves of this and that, on choosing and payment is required, she piles the shit on the conveyer belt and quickly scurries past to bag it up whilst he pays. These items paid for by him and to be installed by him, un paid, she sits on the sofa devouring soap opera, after soap opera, only turning the head at intervals. "come and have a break darling" she mews, this show of compassion due to there being an extremely shocking and powerful happening in the soap she is currently aghast and enthralled in, the break in his unpaid work is not for his benefit, but is surreptitiously manufactured for quiet, so she doesn't have to think about what he is doing wrong, and instead can give her undivided attention to the mind blowing events about to unfold.

So when meeting up at the local Costa (when he is at work) the aforementioned events can be relived and dissected with her bestie (whilst her husband is also at work). He sits on break drinking the tea he made, dunking the biscuits he fetched, and dutifully returns to work after twenty minutes or so, in the local Costa, time is not an issue.

Grass cutting is "unpaid work", mostly done by males, the mower being a somewhat dangerous and unpredictable machine has to be kept under control at all times (not unlike himself), and kept functional with dirty chemicals such as oil, a very unglamorous product (unless, of the virgin olive variety, splashed over salad, when on a leisurely lunch), which in the event of a tragic a accident could soil ones gardening gloves. Then there is the digging, another cumbersome affair, which has to be approached with caution, as a serious wearing of ones self out could occur, weeding, another strange job in need of supervision, to avoid the pulling up or cutting down of incorrect plants, due to his "unpaid work", to offset her lack of physical effort she has to be in total control of the what's and where's, so on praise the garden can be safely claimed as her sole effort, with the throw away comment "he just cuts the grass". She wears the gardening gloves in this house "yes siren bob" and wields those secateurs with precision, as long as he picks up all those prickly branches, as any man should.

Then there is the ownership of garden buildings, the conservatory shared, green house shared, the garden shed is nearly always domain, this is due to it's contents, and it's usually unfeminine dilapidated appearance, once inside an array of tools and chemicals not fit for female use, alongside the odd spider. If the shed is transformed into a lookalike beach hut, with a small veranda that's a different matter, then the space becomes attractive to her, chairs and a small table can be installed, plastic red checked table cloth, plastic pretzel platter and white wine can now be safely consumed on the premises, after a curtain is hung on the shed window to avoid the unsightly contents. The female can now sit and ruminate and dream to aspire to the next level, upon the shirt tails of whom ever will succumb to the contents of her underwear.

The dangerous machinery with in the shed such as the lawnmower with it's ungodly mind of it's own, and the need for fuel and oil, and the change of a spark plug every two years, this could take months of training for her to accomplish these skills, alas the man need not worry about such matters, as she will show no interest any way. If the machine is electric, the avoidance of cutting the cable is essential. We also have the electric hedge trimmer, a machine of such fearsome appearance is enough send any one of a weak disposition scurrying for the latest copy of Hello magazine, accompanied by day time television's goddesses "loose women".

(i am pretty sure, undressed, they would be as loose and more as their name suggests. An obscene sight to go along with the obscene rhetoric and painted faces of these has beens, who command obscene salaries and "carte blanche" impunity to deride any thing of male constructive opinion, not directly designed to improve the impoverished and oppressed female audience in their stinking onesies at two pm in the afternoon).Then at the end of operations the laborious folding of the cable, and placing back in "the shed" a place full of such mystery, the machine is left at the door for later stowage. We have also in some cases a pressure washer to contend with, handy for cleaning cars, patios and mountain bikers, after a ride out with dad.

Then there are the hand tools, which in turn save the household hundreds of pounds every year, wielded and purchased by him alone, "unpaid work" that saves the family money. If any discourse is shown on the mention of a job he needs to be doing, the mantra, "we'll get someone in", and he knows one way or another, he will pay for non-compliance, whether out of his own pocket directly, or the fake joint account, which he deposits 70% she the rest, sometimes. An assortment of screwdrivers, spanners and sockets etc are tidily shelved in "the shed", if such a tool was placed in the hands of a female a look if fear and bewilderment usually with the saying "what am I to do with that" (answers on a postcard please)this is due to the absolute lack of interest in any activity involving the use of such tools. The establishment can try to promote as many policies and set up learning centres and think tanks as they wish, to try to socially engineer what they see as a perfectly normal transition of gender, into a gender neutral work-place. This foolish ideology will never materialise, women do not want to get cold or get their hands dirty, and if both are required to succeed forget it, the powers that be should, own up to the failure of this pipe dream that no women will ever weld, never mind lay on a bed of gravel.

When it comes to domestic machinery the whole scenario changes, these quiet inoffensive washing machines, dryers, some even combined to carry out both tasks, (I suppose this is needed to save time and having to bend ones back twice, to unload the laundry from one machine to the other), the clean and safe use of hoovers or irons was the woman's remit, the choosing of the most expensive appliances in order to be released from this domestic drudgery. Once installed the interest in the said machines begins to fade and disinterest is again the order of the day, and rosters made to empty and fill, for the rest of the family.

The way to reverse any of the aforementioned is to categorically state on eastenders, or loose women, that under no circumstances women would be allowed in "the shed" or use other male implements, then an army of women would storm shed after shed, to maybe construct banners for three year olds on the impending armageddon and block up roads, so men cannot get to work, whilst they flaunt their immature stupidity, and display the childish self serving people they are. If a bill was passed, women only are allowed in the shed, the would never wish to enter, due to the fact women are now forced to take control of "the shed" and all it's contents, the gardens beauty declines, under now a fully female venture, it becomes ugly and unsightly, without the mans toil and endeavour, a scenario played out through many failed state interventions, in the name of progress. Of course it will not be aimed at the females failure to carry the tasks required, a lack of training, for these poor women thrown in at the deep end of mowing and weeding, foul play is at hand, no transparent guidelines were firmly put in place, alongside underfunding, shameful treatment of elite gardeners (who have a cock and balls) is as usual, the demise and mismanagement of most projects, biased towards women, over inclusion at all costs, you do not see Zebra climbing trees.

The understanding that women are pushed out of the workplace is another lie to cover lack of will and competency to name but two, highly qualified, thus I assume highly intelligent women are in fact choosing to opt out. In 1981 a study shows that 1in3 women with an MBA is not working, against 1in20 men, the data suggests these woman are becoming lost assets to the workplace. This notion is scratchy at best, as no one can predict the impact of any woman would have with in the workplace had she remained in that position longer. All the supposition as wether it is beneficial to the employer if she stays or goes is purely subjective, how can you measure if there is a substantial gain or not, but as with all cloudy issues, the benefit will be with her.

In a title of American literature "women of leadership" the data is 37% of women opt and 27% of men do the same, not a huge difference, but the male activity seems (or so they say) to be a lot less worrying for employers, and any mention of male actions are played down if questioned at all. Is it the female inclination to carp on about any difference in any situation should be down to the oppression and not being included (in what "they" want to be included in of course) and unfairly treated and on and on, this is why the female side of this argument trumps the man's.

In a centre of "Work life policy", it was recorded that 40% of highly educated women said the "man did nothing around the house but make a mess", I am pretty sure she relayed this to the cleaner in a second, upon the location of a rogue coffee cup in the bathroom, this act of blatant disregard for any woman's self esteem would be discussed in the salon, which I am sure will be met with disbelief and the nodding of newly coiffured heads.

Lack of interest is another reason cited fo the opt out, what ever position or level women are on does not have the complexities required for them to to tolerate the inconvenience of full time work, these being set hours, and an expectation that one turns up every day, every week, when they are tightly shackled down as most men are, they do not like it. The family commitment is another opt out ticket to the freedom they crave, feet up after taking the kids to school etc etc.

Then a study says there are not many women who have the privilege of not having to work, so why all the bluster about equality, when the thought is for a woman not to work is a "privilege", this all stinks of the hypocrisy which is rarely afforded by men, but only to the female elite club of down trodden females, hard done by in a society of injustice. Of the many women who claim the returning to work is a right of passage and life for filling dream, this is on the understanding she can come and go as she pleases, Flexi-time or part-time or even job sharing, the desire to cherrypick what suits them is the main criteria that must be adhered to in the name of equality and fair play. Another reason to return to work is to bolster up the family coffers, to enhance the family's standing with in the community, or in other terms, to give her more leverage in the amount of the next loan or settee, even though doing a quarter of the hours and little pay being placed in the "joint-account". Some women opt out to do charity work, another hobby with out hard and fast rules to be followed, there wish to do "more meaningful work", this is merely so they can be seen doing "something", when they feel like doing "something", on the return to work, if not full time the pay is less than before, their old job may not exist, so a new post must be invented, if the old position does still exist someone else is carrying it out, and they may happen not be better in this, and will need no special treatment, no doctors appointments etc, is just one the things that come with having children, times move on whether you are at home with a baby or not. The new employee is not there to keep the seat warm, they have their own agendas and needs.

The man is usually the more ambitious concerning work,

and more driven to succeed, unlike women many men want the responsibility that goes with the big salary, so she dutifully allows him his 80 hours a week to fight his way to the top, somewhere she has no wish to be. She benefits directly on his hard earned success, more time with the kids, more time in the wonderful new house, her own credit card for clothes and nails and hair, more time with friends (friends just like her). Then the cry of neglect comes into play "always being at work" is now a crime and things begin to decline, due to his selfish 20 years of 80 hours a week to succeeding make a better life for the around him and the ones he loves most. She has more and more time on manicured hands, a show if interest distracts her, this is interest, this man maybe of "lower standing" than her husband, an unthinkable thought a few years before, but with all the trappings safely in hand this is now not an issue. The incoming male will listen intensively, for as long as necessary, so the trust to remove the knickers is won, (usually not a huge amount of time), feeling safe that she now has some one who cares, the divorce begins, and financial rape of all he has worked for, all fully backed and carefully legislated by the state.

Women will want to work with in a group or "team", to collaborate, this is because any shortfall can be spread amongst the team, and any lack of suitability is disguised, also frequent days of or early finishes, will have less impact on a group then a sole task by a sole employee. In fact the female's desire for part-time is only equal to the male's endeavour to secure over-time, as the financial responsibility, is almost exclusively with the man. If this financial pressure is called out the female will feel undervalued when confronted with the facts, but many who leave their full time occupation, for whatever reason, seldom return to the role fully she held before, these are clearly cases of self-imposed opt out, and not a case of being pushed out, which women are desperate for all to believe, to some way cover up lack of drive in life, and succumbing to being a kept woman, such an idea is fiercely denied. The upshot of all this is to form a carefully worked strategy to give the woman the best of both worlds, and when they feel that's not so another strategy will be required, and all the feeble males and the state will do all they can to enable this to happen.

What else could she possible want, paying for staying at home, that's been on the cards for a while now, surly one day this will be implemented at huge cost and again the enforcement of her well being trumps the male. Free housing, many already have that, hardly any male lives in free housing, the nearest thing to that is a hostel, shared by many like himself, very rare by females. All women shortlists, in all aspects of life, apart from any thing physical or mentally demanding, because the danger here for women, with all this bias in their favour, they may actually get the job, and if they get the job, she can no longer claim being a woman has hampered a path to success, in any way, the opposite in many cases is at play.

When all senior government posts, and private company senior posts, alongside all institutions in the world that women see exclusively dominated by men, accept the ones that women show no interest in, (manual construction work being one), when all these posts are filled with dynamic superhuman females, handed over on a plate by All Women Shortlists or any other devious means they wish to employ, how will the women cope. The answer, they won't, for many varied reasons, if you destabilise any situation that is functioning by force rarely has a good outcome, for a short time maybe, how will the woman react to lack of experience and responsibility, the day to day dealing with personnel, the female propensity to cry when compromised would hardly in still trust and respect within the workforce. Their inability to separate home-life and work-life, the huge amount of hours required to maintain a positions of the magnitude these top jobs demand, cannot be compromised by family issues, a family photo on the office desk is as far as it gets sometimes, women are more likely to crumble under the savage pressure of hard nosed business, the menstrual cycle can make their temperament fluctuate beyond reason or control, the menopause is another factor, all this has to be so, or women would not spend half their lives whittling on that men do not have to suffer the biological tsunamis they have to endure on a, weekly, monthly basis. Does this sound like a logical reason to shoe horn women into critical jobs they are simply not suitable for, they would already be filling these posts if it was just an academic matter, which in some cases women have shown their capability of reaching the standard required, but their is much more to it as to why in most cases men prevail.

Then the complicated matter of having children during and after the pregnancy are with out doubt difficult and demanding times, no matter how one plans it all out, how could the head of a company disappear for 11 months then expect to to the same position, even at Mackie Dees flipping burgers the same dynamic exists, or will the blind equality laws legislate, that she must be allowed to return on the same footing when she left, to which the whole house of cards will come tumbling down, for the simple reason business and life are never stationary, change occurs or the situation or business fails to compete. Whilst "on leave" up to her elbows in fairy liquid and copies of mother and baby magazines no matter how many video conferences she attends, working from home doesn't cut it. With all the best will in the world you cannot champion industry or any other career of a certain level, propped up on your Gratton suit in the conservatory with your laptop, even if some one else is changing nappies for you.

When top flight questions need to be answered and a strategy put in place how will the women perform, well known for drawn out conversations in any sphere of life, being in control of the avoidance of company pitfalls and multi-million pound contracts to negotiate, on time, and their ability to make decisions with out the luxury of having some one else to blame in the event of catastrophe, would be difficult for them to say the least, all of this unnecessary pressure when a good living can be made fiddling the house keeping and stealing out of the husbands pockets when he comes home pist. It will be interesting to see how career women evolve out there in the open market in positions once held by men without all the isms in place to protect them, and sexism is at the back of the due. Men are willing to sacrifice every thing for a successful high end career, this notion of life balance and have it all mums, is frankly for the birds. To sacrifice and fore sake the the family, friends, and in some cases physical health and mental health is one hell of a commitment, we can all name top business women of course they exist, but the balance 50% men 50% women will never exist, as more men will go through the required demands than women. So to destroy the status quo in the name of "need for change" and no other reason, will be a huge financial mistake to the economy and we all suffer for an experiment of social leftwing ideas, when the women have failed, and you bet it will not be their fault, they will slink away with huge pay offs, and leave the men who have been overlooked due to quotas and bias, to sort the whole mess out, to whom they will blame the mess on the position taken over, by default, was in such a mess left by men, it was impossible to succeed. The limited resource of super women is an on going phenomenon that will last and last, with successful men come successful wives, who marry into a financial bracket above their own, rarely below as most men have to, with the woman's financial security in place comes time, they can train and venture into any little cottage industries, write books become doyennes of all before them, all on the back of their husbands finances. The ability to fail is for all, but the confidence for women to try such things is only there because the financial repercussions will be his. The problem with sole control and responsibility and no one to point the diamond encrusted finger at, with may be many employees livelihoods at risk, the hunger for success will evaporate and a quick retreat to the country spa required. There is no question of ability, just the question of suitability and dogged will power, I think this is a big, big ask, for women who are used to having it easy.

The office of national statistics 2013 says 1% of mechanics are female, and 93% of dental nurses are female, this in it's self tells us all we know, but never say, women like clean easy jobs, that do not start before 9am, and leave the dirty work to men. Social workers are 82% female, in civil engineering 11% are women, of which 90% are pen pushers, with clip boards tightly clutched to their chests. 99% of bricklayers are men, why does this ridiculous notion women want to be in construction, workplace equality costs millions of pounds all for what, women with beaming smiles on posters in their brand new Personnel Protection Equipment, never to be soiled in the name of work, unless they fall over on site, they hold if a little awkwardly shiny new and brick in hand, all of this I the name of something they never want to part of in the first place, all this is about as plausible as employing chickens to stake shelfs in the local super market (no disrespect to chickens intended).

With the huge disproportionate number of women in the Social Work sector, how can a balanced approach and out come be so, with hardly any male input. As the issues of families is the remit how can this be fair, as fifty percent of the nation are men. Of course feminists hold the posts which maintain this huge imbalance of gender, I hear no cry of diversity, quotas all male short lists. How has it been kept about the same numbers are employed for the last thirty years.

I have yet to hear any investigation of mistakes and shortfalls, not to mention many deaths of of innocent children, laid at the door of gender imbalance and lack of inclusivity, all these very important issues effect men and women equally, and stop stigmatising men when applying for these jobs. Alas in all matters concerning diversity, inclusivity and short listings only apply to females, or so it seems.

CHAPTER FOUR

In divorce why is it that after two appearances, if an agreement cannot be reached, regarding of course, the financial settlement (why else would any one be there, wife gets paid, judge gets paid, legal team gets paid (usually wife and husbands legal teams by him), in the event of a third hearing, the judge has sole control of the outcome, In a situation of insurmountable importance how can this be correct, the pressure will always be put on the one with most to loose, "if you can't agree, the judge will decide, and that could be worse, for you",. I am sure there are some sort of guidelines the judge must follow, even if they are from 1974, and again in almost total favour of the woman, in all this the man is on a tightrope of emotions that will seal his fate for the unseeable future, and in many cases he feels the only way out, is suicide. It has become high fashion to, demean, discredit and disentangle the husband from all he has fought and toiled for in an instant, on a whim, of some person who has, and has no interest in knowing, in depth of the circumstances, of which they preside over, other than "were is the money". This detachment from all relevant information, must surly have a detrimental effect on the outcome, of which in nearly all cases the husband gets a kicking. The stay at home mum, promised fortunes, and starry eyes, the thought of a spending spree previously unheard of, shackled in the shops by "him", now a chance to get "their" money and do what she wants with it, bright eyed solicitors uncover financial rewards, before unknown to exist, because they don't, the house, half each, somewhere to live is a necessity not an asset, and mostly he will suffer, pensions cut short and made worthless, any liquid assets liquidated, in her favour.

The input of the stay at home wife, is never in question, an admirable life choice of huge importance, so the outcome of the child's suitability to join humanity, must be mainly influenced by the mother in the most important, early years. So if the child is a complete fuck up, should she be paid for this dereliction of duty, should the court take into consideration if she has kept herself in good order, check the bookshelves for dust, all these things are her side of the contract, if he has dutifully amassed the family fortune solely on his employment, thus fore filling his role as provider, why should the spoils be in her favour, only the court can explain. The explanation, is based, on future needs, supposition, the woman's lack of competence in being able to support the family without his input, or even support herself is at best questionable, so even before she fails, the court work on the assumption she will, and again he must pay, no other case of law would be dealt in this manner, but divorce is a stand alone branch of law, and will never be changed, due to the lucrative nature and ease of which it has full control to steal and loot men at will, all the politically correct brigade, the left, and feminists etc etc of course support and commend every broken man in the name of equality.

The bible says: Ecclesiastes: 4.9. two are better than one, because they have a good return on their labour.

We are no longer walking side by side happily scattering seeds together, in a rendition frequented with in the pages of Watchtower or Awake, tell a bricklayer four lifts up on a windy winter morning, how his wife sitting home watching television, is a good return on his labour.

Ephesians: husbands love your wife give up your life for her. These types of suggestions do nothing to inspire young men, and in many brutal divorce cases the men do indeed give their lives up, unfortunately.

With the timely invention of metro-sexual man the labour of child care and housework have become somewhat blurred and fudged to a point of how an earth could a complete stranger, no matter how erudite and professional they seem, could have a scintilla of hope to unravel the endeavours of either party over a lengthy period of time, never mind put a cost on it. There is no need to worry about this, because the man or woman judge can simply file their arms, and with an indifferent manner proclaim 50 50, is the outcome.

Now the sixty year old man no use for work never mind fucking, mind bent and buckled, all hope devoured by the state, no fight left only demise of a once proud, resilient member of society belittled and beaten down by the in-equality of the law, in a way so brutal, if witnessed in a third world country, this would sit alongside the adverts for save the donkeys and life insurance on day time television, if it was not almost exclusively tailored to suit over weight underworked females who dwell in a dimension alien to most men. The strange wish to see and enforce the battering down of the male population, and to downgrade them to the position the women feel that once they had to endure, is ridiculous, and incorrect. The image of the suffragettes (what a stupid word), these grimy victorian events, shrouded in pain and torment, not by women only most people were cold in the winter and hungry all year around men and women and children.

The will to impose pain and misery on other women's sons, and in a twisted way their own, is another show of the so called desperate struggle they feel over powers all things, even the ones they are not interested in. I find a similarity in big game hunting, now illegal, the stalking of a quarry, which to all intense and purpose, has been cultivated to enhance the hunters odds, so the deplorable act can be executed, sitting on or holding the head up of a once majestic beast, is no less disturbing than the outcome a modern divorce court.

My first experience, of the state of play with in the divorce phenomenon was being instructed to buy a lottery ticket and cross my fingers, this was by the owner of the practice. This was a thunderbolt, but only one of many to come, this sickened me and I felt extremely fearful of my future, when the word of a professional in the field, that is there to protect justice for all, seems to ignore the actuality of the phenomenon, or in legal terms, fully endorses the criminal deceit, intent and conduct, when one tries to justify the outcome of the vast majority of divorce cases.

The message from my first encounter was, when I asked about the fairness of justice, he smiled and replied, " justice, oh no, you will not get justice, you will get the law".

As previously mentioned, in the event of a stalemate, the judge has the final say, it must be questionable, as to how, without a jury, can a fair result be obtained. How can he or she pass a life changing decision on people so little is known about, the guidelines are there, but the judge must ultimately ruling from a personnel point of view, this can never be correct, everyone has agendas which may impinge in a detrimental way, these hidden agendas are to ensure the woman is looked after, for all said and done, it's human instinct to protect the weak. It would be pure folly to suggest that, with which genitalia you are born with, will in decades to come, decide as to wether you are made or slayed, in the modern divorce courts, but this is the outcome for all to see, across the land. All of this is nothing other than a contradiction, contractually binding everyone by the law of the law, the pro's and con's are most certainly examined and evaluated in all cases, other than the format of divorce. This wave of the hand to all mitigating circumstances, is not without reason, if there is no money (his money) nobody will get paid, so the question is, "where is the money". One wonders why all the cases presided over by a summary judge, would not benefit with a jury, this would make the outcome fairer, purely on the diversity of opinion.

The divorce system in the court room has stagnated, to the males detriment, if this was to the females detriment, no doubt change would be demanded, and sooner or later change would be upon us, with endless protests by scruffy overweight couch potatoes, waving home made, mis- spelt banners, in novelty t-shirts littering the capitals streets. Misrepresentation and deception and fraud are all criminal offences, punishable by financial or custodial penalties, in divorce this hardly ever occurs, this is due to the male usually getting the raw deal, and any offences committed by the woman are overlooked. This comparison of standards is freely available, daily, in any red top.

Still the vast majority of divorce cases initiated by disturbed women, are quite simply conducted from all angles in an unfair manner from the off, biased and with out any mercy shown to the husband. Indeed it is so outrageous and unbalanced (one of the main replies to my own dilemma, was, "they can't do that". "oh yes they can" was my reply, "it's the law"), these so called legal proceedings are delivered without sense or reason, any person with an ounce of morality, would be non-plussed at the total destruction perpetrated in the name of the law, bye the say so of some demented plaintiff. It is undeniable that the ex-wife in her new found boundless energy, in the newly acquired power over the man she once loved, and now hates with more passion than she ever loved, this limitless financial power is mesmerising for her, hell bent on annihilation of the person once taken for "better or worse", looking dewy eyed into a face now unrecognisable, due to the relentless path, these once timid and tortured beasts have embarked on, they hack and gouge their way to be the custodian of his wealth, fully backed by the law and state. Despite the tens of thousands of men looking for a common sense explanation as to why such a contemptible state of legal in-equality not only exists, but thrives, and the most consistent answer being "i know it's wrong but".

There is a clear reason many middle aged men suffer from alcohol issues and mental health problems, it is due to the hole the establishment and society and the law, have found it necessary to throw them in, and keep their foot firmly upon the heads of these depressed and oppressed members of society. The lack of help and interest in these men, who not surprisingly are the most likely to commit suicide, is shocking and deplorable, this is because this group of men are simply not trendy enough to qualify for support, as the pink haired fat tattooed lesbians, or the transvestite getting his lacy knickers in a twist after getting the sack from the local charity shop, because his deep voice is scaring the customers not to mention huge hairy hands and ill fitting wig. Conjure up those images, and then the image a grey haired (if any)middle aged man, in saggy arsed jeans, dirty white trainers, with the smell of alcohol on his breath, the only support is to tell him "pull yourself together", which is a huge insult to a man on the edge of reason, and in some cases send him to the nearest bridge. These men are almost exclusively members of the same club, set up and run by the state, this pitiful club, one of the membership criteria is usually a spell in the divorce court, who's dogged determination make men pay for all they have, or haven't done, through antiquated laws over half a century old. Thrown out of homes, they owned a decade before the marriage, and are the sole up-keeper still, on the whim of a judge, chest puffed out in doing the right thing mode, no knowledge of the circumstances, if any are introduced, they are swatted away with impunity, again all that matters is "were is the money", every one needs to get paid, a third to her a third to us and leave him a third, less all costs and what ever else needs to be paid. This leaves the man stateless, in the confusion he is lost. This may lead to unemployment, homelessness, degraded from all sides, their identity shredded by the people also known as the authorities, have washed their hands of these men and pulled the plug out.

The machinations of these so called better halves, are early deployed upon a son, father or brother, possibly because one of their like is already doing it, or even more likely due to the non backing of the state, in not fully backing them in breaking of family members, unethical maybe, but is more than happy to indulge in the destruction a husband, with financial reparation a must.

The first step is to deny any physical contact, or if it is allowed, the circumstance and length of time must be fully under her control, and must be initiated by him, to make him feel it is he and only he who needs tis contact, she must also show discomfort in letting this act transpire, all of this is the woman telling him I will tolerate you for now, but I don't want you, this is just where she wants him. The joint-bank account, is now the key, all monies must be scrutinised and calculated, so on the conclusion of the final deception in the divorce court all monies will be secured. One of the most ironic things is the mantra from the start of the relationship, " I don't care about your money" time and time again, then at the death the opposite, it's all they care about, again a shameless u-turn, purely down to greed.

Then the decamping from the big bed to the spare room or if not available the settee, when asked by the children, the embarrassed father makes excuses, like it's his snoring. Once evicted permanently from the master bedroom the next step is to gain control of the children minds, with out and out lies, in order to make the children feel she cares about their dad and " it's for the best and she still loves him, but not like that any more", this abuse of compassion and lack of empathy shown towards the children is of a psychopathic nature, this is just the start of the process to destroy the family and annihilate the father. In years gone by the main family dwelling was council owned, then introduced by one of the greatest women who ever lived Margret Thatcher, the right to buy came into play, she knew if you never paid the rent, the council would huff and puff but little else, the bank on an outstanding mortgage is a different matter. This was also a very clever ploy to shackle the man to 25 years of hard labour, after which many men came away with nothing and many women came away with everything. The down side to home ownership was to set the seed for ultimate greed and indifference, that any human being can show to another, backed by a greedy lawyers, this is the main asset in most divorces. If all attempts by her to get him to leave his house, his home, lies must be employed, and defamation of character, the two most ambiguous are domestic violence and alcohol abuse, both of these can be an accusation, with no physical proof, but the police will remove the man any way. If he resists an already harrowing sight for the children, handcuffed and arrested inside the family home, this may well be the last time the children see dad inside the place they grew up together.

Now she has the house and the kids, and all the benefits that literally go with it, the single mother tag they wear with pride "i brought the kids up alone", er no you didn't, the state clothed and fed them, educated them looked after their welfare, not to mention maintenance payments by the father on the outside looking in, made to look like a deserter, when she puts in place, the visitation restraints, backed by the state, many men give up due to the hubris surrounding the whole affair. Then the establishment steps in with The Child Support Agency, responsible for the murder of countless innocent men across the land, in doing this they take away the father from the children they claim to champion. When she cashes in the life insurance, she can lavish gifts on herself and the kids, but only she knows where the money came from, and why all this was necessary, but she is still self-serving enough to spend a dead man's money.

A set of amendments were to be made to the divorce acts laws, on fairness of financial matters, to be discussed, among many other things, was the enrichment of one party (almost always the wife), to the detriment of the other (almost always the man). In the out set this was never to be, the unwillingness, down to the fact, that if you remove the financial burden (her), then someone else will have to pick up the bill, in this case, it would go from him to the state, now the state cannot allow that to happen, billions of pounds plundered from honest men, to be replaced by billions of pounds paid out by the state, who actually engineered the whole problem. Alas for millions of men looking for a little parity, a night I shining armour came thundering over the hill to save the state this costly exercise. This saviours name "Brexit" no less, so any progress was conveniently shelved, as parliamentary time was in short supply for such trivial matters as the the obliteration of millions of men's finances, so it continues. So any man who "has done alright for himself" must continue with no questions asked, literally, with all the states platitudes in abundance and firmly in place, the upshot, don't expect change anytime soon. All the greedy wives out there can heave a heavy sigh of relief, if aware of theses circumstances, many are ignorant of most political matters, other than climate change, extinction rebellion, black lives matter, and any other organisation that has nothing to do with payments they hoover up every month, as long as every time they stretch out that well manicured mit, it is crossed with silver, why would they care about the legitimacy of whence it came. Only when this money tree stops shaking does the federal case begin, and all men must be slain and disembowelled, in order to reinstate the financial status quo.

The law to stem the systematic abuse of husbands will never be given serious thought by the ones who should know better, the judiciary, far to much money is made of the back of these men, nailed to the cross of gold, shrouded in complicated text and clandestine discussions between those who enjoy the spoils of misery, who benefit directly by prolonging the cases, solicitors get the first bite, then usually on the recommendation of the solicitor, the second hearing will require the golden pigs, the barrister, minimum 2000 pounds a day plus VAT, . In what other scenario would any person contemplate this gargantuan payment for two maybe three hours service, the desperate, that's who, those desperate to gain, those desperate not to loose everything. These legal teams of professional tyrants, steal and destroy the very notion of justice, flitting in between government financed well heated rooms, the outcome never in doubt, "where is the money", the judge sitting in the ivory tower of power over all matters, no out come the third court date may loom and threaten even more financial destruction, so to up the ante is out of the question, as the mortified recipient (usually the man) puts their cards on the table and looks away. Their seems to be, due to the huge financial rewards along with the ease of the nature of the work, after all it is already written down in those in thick tomes, on the shelves behind these legal eagles, they thumb through these ancient scrolls to trip and turn events in the favour of who ever is paying, many women are now entering the profession, which can only lead to a partizan attitude, wether meant or subconscious is irrelevant, the outcome is the same, men get shafted.

Another extremely unfair condition is if the wife is of a different tongue, and any documents need to be translated, that directly concern the divorce, well the settlement I mean, the divorce is a secondary goal, no one gets paid if the settlement is not satisfactory to all, but those who made the money, if the wife declares she has no funds, the judge will then order the husband to pay half of any costs incurred. I can only surmise that this is another way to bare down financially on the husband, in a hope he will throw the keys on the table, and shut the door on the way out. All the assets and cash he has earned in his own country, can be mopped up and moved to another country, and be secreted into their economy to the detriment of our own, this runs into hundreds of millions of pounds, the exact amount will never be known, or cared about, due to it happens to mainly men, all of this exchanging of funds fully rubber stamped by the state, in the euphoria of doing the write thing (for women) against the right people (men).

So, the gravy train thunders on through the countryside to the next port of call, with it's female passengers waving the life long free rail tickets, out of half open windows, to the men bent double toiling in the fields. Sat in the first class, plush cabins of life, the service never ceases, the food and drinks, free of charge, served by gaunt divorcees, who's only crime was to be born a man, the women's snide remarks from furry faces is only cut short, to enable a surreptitious glance sideways, to make sure the others do not have more on their plates than she. It would take a Herculean effort to halt this free ride of free loaders, due the tickets are freely available, sponsored by the state, with law after law put in place to make sure of the continuation. When laws are made to favour one group against another, that is shown to have been a mistake, takes much longer to repeal than enact, especially with the modern trend to favour women over men, this maybe due to more women involved with in the legal system, and men forced to think like women in order to hold on to very lucrative jobs, this tact is a very poor show, when you are paid by the public, and above all have the publics interest paramount.

To get a pampered sow's nose out of the trough is a difficult and precarious task, as they are constantly hungry, complex measures need to be employed, the tactic of diversion is essential.

The embarkation on a journey of blowing smoke up arses is required, to say what a wonderful advancement has been madly the females, since the seventies, in the workplace and above all the financial equality we have nearly achieved, is nothing short of a miracle, do the women not agree, if so, maybe a little fairness would not go amiss in the divorce courts, now this bright new age is upon us. This acknowledgement will be hard to find, as enough is never enough, to remove the pigs from the trough, and the passengers from the gravy train will take a tectonic shift, to level up the playing field. Laws can be re-written and reassessed with our wonderful legal system, the envy of the world ?,until it comes to fairness of financial matters after divorce, in this we are firmly ensconced in the early seventies, with no change in sight, the financial burden is to great to be transferred to the state, so innocent men, fathers, brothers and sons are forced into the only option of freedom, self-imposed death, nothing short of state execution. With full knowledge of all the facts and statistics and reasonings, the state continues on the same path, time and time again, this in itself must be seen as premeditated state murder. The only way to the gravy trains, is for the men to stop building them, the woman will never take over such dirty work, and stop filling the troughs with to much food, to force the sows to move away and exploit another source.

There is no logic or jury halt the outrageous demands, and pathetic whys, and wherefores it is pretty obvious most cases would be dismantled, with the intervention a body of people with no legal knowledge to influence them, to apply a commodity well out of date in these politically correct times, common sense. The act of demonising men and stripping them of their assets, with excuse of the law, is unjust and in need of urgent reform. I am sure this systematic destruction and oppression of men, fully supported by the state, in one of the most liberal countries in the world, will in the future be looked upon, in the same view as slavery, and the holocaust, with the plight of the suffragettes coming a very poor runner up. The relentless law making and hiding the truth (women call this groundbreaking reform) will in the future be scrutinised, and exposed for what it is, an extremely distasteful and corrosive part of our past, that was ultimately responsible for the detrimental effects on the father, thus the relationship with his children damage beyond repair alongside his own well being.

Hoorah, the afternoon wine glasses chink in the air, held aloft as the day slowly slips gently by, another divorce party curtesy of the state, the self-serving heaps of seated flesh celebrate, for the last 30 years of a financial bonanza, created by the state, and backed by well meaning male dunderheads. With property confiscated and handed on a plate to un-deserving women, who exhibit an air of impunity, seldom shown by a man, because he knows the cost of 90% of all things, his name is on the bill, she doesn't know the cost, or wants to know, she doesn't need to, she's not paying. With the relentless pursuit of "where is the money" (his money), no shame or empathy will be shown, the false cry "it's for the children" resonates, this onslaught of depravity is never questioned or even acknowledged, due to the disdain and total disrespect shown by the state, to these fathers trying to do the right thing. These human beings are not expendable or to be seen as collateral damage in a society skewed in the favour, of a breed, far more feckless, who show contempt beyond belief, that any man could not even muster. Eventually he is crushed and broken beyond repair, when of no financial use, she turns to the state, who gladly step up with heart felt sincerity, and great joy to be of assistance, another organisation, social services, ran by women for women.

In any contract of worth there are two components, scope of work and specifics, until these are incorporated in marriage and more importantly the hard nosed business of divorce, the man has no chance of a fair outcome. This would in some way unravel the ambiguity at the end of the marriage, and instead of the cry "where is the money" into "who made the money, and how much contribution was made to enable this to happen", this in most cases would bring an end to the financial ruin of men, through no fault of their own. When these two parts of the contract are firmly embedded into the law of marriage, and only then will the level playing be reached. When all aspects and numbers have been squared and agreed and signed can the union of marriage be granted. The woman will obviously object to any of this, claiming it will taint "the big day" (her big day), she will insist must only involve trust and love, both of which are never found in the divorce court. After the 2000 pound dresses, have been long packed away, the flowers have died and the posh cars on rent to the next victims, the mawkish speeches, for the bride have long been silenced, it's time to realise this contract newly entered, is more serious and see through the pathetic opulence and sheer disregard for money, almost entirely at the behest of the woman, that is why the cost of the wedding, should be one of the specifics taken into account, and offset any payment the man has to make. Another reason she will fight tooth and manicured nails to resist the marriage be bought in line with any other normal business contract, is because she is marrying into a better financial position, then she is at present, she is in a no loss situation (how many men would enter into such a contract at all risk on them). It is never the less astounding, that the law of specifics and scope of work have been overlooked by the man, this is purely the result of the female never wanting to discuss the dirty subject of money, until the contract is sealed, again how many contracts would he enter blind on a normal business footing, all these matters are not her point of view, so her view point must be allowed to overrule all the rules, because, it's her big day, and any mention of any thing to her dislike must be quashed immediately in order for the big day to go smoothly with out floods of tears. If only some integrity was sown in the marriage, the maybe the divorce out come would be a little fairer.

In the event of divorce, the amount of work done, monies put in, monies taken out, and for what use, and also what has been achieved with in the time-line of the marriage. Willingness to extend ones self when ever required, willingness to be flexible, willingness to take risks in the workplace to maximise earnings, these traits are mostly male, also the physical and mental cost of being out of your comfort zone, has on the man. Unless the woman finds a job that suits her lifestyle, and hours she is willing to give up, and has no work involved, and only then will she pursue the post with vigour, until a little responsibility rears it's ugly head.

In the marriage ceremony the specifics are all unmeasurable, and the fantasy ideology it rests upon, love and trust. Maybe, as in a driving test, there should be theory test on specifics, before the ceremony it's self, when all the specifics are understood and agreed and any prenuptial agreements signed off, can the contract of marriage be fully binding. As in the driving test many fully understand the theory side, but have great difficulty in the practical side. Non of the above will ever come into being, due to the machinations and dogma that the women will employ at all costs, to remove any chance of the chattels and finances be out of their reach, the man knows what is expected of him, and blindly continues to follow the well trodden path of the well trodden.

This complete refusal to have a pragmatic discussion about money, should be his wake up call, and give him valuable insight into the future behaviour of the one he is about to marry.

The main reason that the prenuptial agreements are invalid in this country seems to be the mis- conception, that through no fault of her own she won't get her hands on what he already had, it is said by the powers that be, the economically weaker spouse will suffer (her), and being more vulnerable, and will be open to negative coercion. To me each spouse should keep what they had prior to wedlock, this to any sensible person is just and fair (not in the woman's eyes, as she mostly brings fuck all into the marriage), and to suggest either party would suffer if the assets previously owned were out of bounds, is for the birds (feathered and non-feathered). Also the prenuptial agreements must be in place with in a certain time before the marriage ceremony, if it is to close she may become flustered about getting her weight down, so the maids of dis-honour can shoe horn her into the sacred garment and tell her how wonderful she looks, these logistical matters over ride any such piffling financial ones. Again all financial matters are irrelevant to her and met with complete indifference, because it is not her money on the line.

Another anomaly in divorce is any debts must be shared and both liable for the full amount, we can only surmise who will be saddled with the debt, and of course in the main it won't be her.

Then there is the term Ancillary Relief, this means usually the man has to subsidise the needs of the woman, a charitable and fanciful way to solve the finances of one person (her) at the cost of (him), non of these hidden clauses ever benefit the man.

Mitigation, is almost non-existent in the financial settlement after divorce, the only constant is "where is the money". Of course no legal professional will admit this (only behind closed doors) the simple fact of the matter, if no money exists, the case does not exist, if there is no money how will everyone get paid, why would the legal teams bother, believe me they won't, in the funds available, usually his, are insufficient the case in the eyes of the so called judiciary is a dead duck.

These legal Dick Turpins hide behind the flimsy mantra "it's the law", that is the biggest cop out within the whole system, in my opinion, divorce law is just a poor subsidiary, without any moral credibility whatsoever. As the divorce court thrives on a set of anomalies that will never be contested, due to the fact that the state knows the financial catastrophe that would ensue, with the responsibility to re-house and finance hundreds of thousands of partners, mainly women. The gender based format is flawed, although clearly evident, just speak to any of the army of men, who have suffered most, lost everything, the very men who's lives have been shattered by the state supported annihilation, of course this has never been documented or made public in a manner we can all understand, with stand alone figures and percentages.if ever this information was put out clearly in the public domain, there would be a serious wake up call, to the men sleepwalking into the dark places life has to offer, free of charge, this is the only fee many of these men will be able to afford.

Legal aid for divorce was all but withdrawn in 2012, much to the dismay of mainly women, as it was almost exclusively devised for their needs, after this safety blanket was stripped away, the women had to fund there own cases, no win no fee practises are supposedly barred from representing any one involved in a divorce case, if this was not so, I am sure they would all back the women, a return to the outdated legal aid funnily enough. So it goes something like this, one third of the money to her needs, one third to the legal teams and judge, the last third minus costs goes to him, they all gain a third, he looses two thirds, plus any pensions in the future to be shared with her, only the liquid assets are of any use, it's now the money needs to be realised and an immediate fiscal settlement obtained, or the dreaded compound interest may be deployed, the legal teams want the money, now. The system needs a complete overhaul, but never will be due to the aforementioned, and the attitude of "where is the money"and "it's the law" need to be changed, two immature statements by people, who frankly should know better.

Even after the spouse is made homeless (usually the man) and orders slapped on him to continue to pay the mortgage and utilities, alongside his own housing needs, with the agreement that when the children reach a certain age the house will be sold and the proceeds shared. After he has honoured all agreements the time comes to sell, she can go back to court and broker another deal for her needs, after living rent free and him still responsible for the wall paper, she again has the last word the state will make sure of that. As we all know this house sale in many cases never transpires, as the man has usually moved on, forging a new life and successful enough to re-home himself and probably stupidly enough with another woman, and the cycle repeats, unless of course he has taken his own life.

Pensions are another way in which the courts can inflict more misery, after an arduous career he may well have despised for the last thirty years for the sole purpose of supporting his family, the pension accrued under year after year of torture is now to be seen as another golden egg to be halved. With all of this persistent badgering by the court in the name of equality, no facility for appeal and as always mitigating circumstances brushed aside, the kids left ten years ago, she lays on the settee swigging gin all day, why, because she can, which again shows, if a contract was in place, a fair outcome could be brokered. Him working five days a week for twenty years, her on the settee for the same, how in any circumstances can this be fair and equal, only the most deranged, along with nazi like gender bias could argue that's so. The pension being one of the major factors in considering a position, as in the case of the public sector the risk takers as in most tings are men, more likely to join the police force or fire service, alongside the odd token woman, who has to be carefully wrapped in cotton wool, to avoid any lawsuits, these hazardous careers pay more, thus more pension, than say a librarian, so in the event of divorce, how can it be fair to again lump every thing together, with complete disregard for any mitigating evidence.

Surly the danger alone, putting ones life on the line, should be reason enough to yield greater recompense, to any lay man or lay woman even, this is glaringly obvious. That is until in the cosy court where equality is blind and savagely upheld, and the art of reason banished long ago, for only one motive, to take from him to give to her. Would this be so if all policemen and firemen, were policewomen and firewomen, of course not, this would have the females pensions safely excluded from male claim, as was in bygone era where men's shielded, until the law felt it necessary for change as in most changes in the woman favour, will this gender imbalance be ironed out in the forces, no, so the divorce court can rob and plunder men's lives with impunity.

The divorce court reminds me of an old fashioned dark room, manned entirely by women, who never shot the photos, but decide which images will be kept and which discarded. This is a summary execution. On 30 years of a man's life, for the sake of equality, the term financial abuse, is coined mainly men against women, when will this desecration of a man's assets at the end of the marriage, be viewed as the same.

CHAPTER FIVE

In modern times with women constructing and de-constructing, anything they feel is not to their benefit, it is astonishing what little progress they have made, or do most of them, not really care or believe in, and even want what the others are continuously crowing about. You can quote facts and figures all day long, but there is no substitute for the observation of everyday life, that is always available, for all of us who want to see it. The major obstacle is the few elite, establishment jobs, hung on by the unanswerable, are portraying incorrect achievable notions, alongside soap operas and reality shows, giving women unobtainable expectations, with apparent consummate ease, due to the one reason being, they are women. When the achievements fall short, there is an army of people pleasers to tell the women it's not their fault, this makes the whole situation worse because the women believe it, it is no coincidence that most of the historical inventors, biologists, mathematicians etc, etc were men, and by the way still are.

The re-invention of historical female figures also essential to the modern myth, and the constructing of a female superiority with out right lies and unearned embellishments, to justify this entourage of inadequates of the now, to see them selves as the best at everything that requires nothing, and needing a steep slope on the playing field, to even achieve this.

Cleopatras is I believe one of these such women, for such a huge figure in history, no one can say how she really looked, if she was black, white, ugly or beautiful, Plutark was to be one of many to describe her as having, ordinary looks, also a coin showed her as hook nosed with bulbous eyes. This sexy svelte figure of beauty, big brown eyes and jet black bob hair cut, emerging from a huge golden bath of milk, was Hollywood fiction at it's best, even better was the superb Carry On Cleopatra, Sid James and crew were probably nearer historical truth than most other depictions. Cleopatra's, apparent willingness to disrobe at any chance to overcome any internal or external threat to national security, wether committing incest or a murderous act against kid sister Asinimi, does not blemish this character which Cleopatra appears to herald, as this persona of compassion and people's person at all levels. She was also credited as being a sage, and philosopher, said to have held court with other muslim leaders, I think not, modern day Muslim leaders find it hard allow female inclusion now, I find it hard to believe this was the case 2000 years ago, some of which her modern day sisters will disagree. Since Carter himself plundered the tombs in The Vally of the Kings, female academics across the world desperate, for some kind of icon to look up to have fought a propaganda war to establish Cleopatra as the main protagonist of the time, ahead of all others, almost all men, is some what hard to swallow, due to her reliance on the thing she was born with, to benefit her people, admirable I am sure, but let us not get to carried way with the notion of her standing, it was more the fruits of her laying. After the marriage to Ceasar, the classic muse and Svengali scenario, she 22 he 52, the rather romantic muse and Svengali is easily explained, the muse wants what usually takes considerable time to obtain, money, thus the Svengali is always a lot older, also the sharing of the man's power is very important, as in Cleopatra's case this power of Ceasar's enabled her to rule Egypt and beyond.

After the murder of Ceasar, Cleopatra sidled up to Marc Antony, for the very same reasoning, and with arguably with more success, three children later, who were ensconced in other lands due to his and his alone influence, and military victories. Cleopatra has also been accredited with being an author of important tomes, by her fawning masses, which collectively arrive at one, the subject cosmetics, claimed to be of scientific importance, there is no real evidence or artefacts to support any of the academic success she is said to have acquired, all is only hearsay and myth, unfortunately this has become common place in our history.

Then we have the acclaimed aviator (balloonist) Sophie Blanchard, who used many aliases for some unknown reason, her luck was to marry a real pioneer, Jean Pierre Blanchard. Who died in a ballooning accident, which was the catalyst that enabled her to take over all her husband's expertise, to self-promote a lucrative career, on the novelty of being a female, all inspiring, all conquering first female aviator, even made into a Hollywood movie, which I have yet to see. She was said to be a small woman of a nervous disposition, which flies in the face of the endeavours that have written, wrongly or rightly this needs to be addressed. As for her influence over Napoleon, and her deployment as The Chief Air Minister, and to oversee an aerial invasion of Great Britain is some what cloudy at best. I am sure these claims have elements of truth, but the fanciful crossing of the Alps maybe one claim to many, even if documented by one such as David J Shaler. The use of basic pyrotechnics (along with throwing dogs out, of the balloon, with parachutes on) was an odd thing to do, due to the fact the balloon relied on flammable gas to enable flight, was to be her undoing. To say the crowd would become restless, if the spectacle wasn't up to expectation, and drove her to take more risks, is again the attempt to compromise female culpability and shift responsibility to the crowd, who I assume some were women. The balloon, was said burst into flames and her demise was complete, on her death a collection was made, an impressive, for the time of 2400 francs, this was for her children, the truth, she had no children, how could a matriarch of her fame and political importance have been so misread.

Hedy Lamarr invented WI-FI was the headline that filled

me with disbelief rarely felt, this is a headline quoted but never questioned in the smudging of history, that is hardly ever used in the chronicling of male history (unless in a negative manner) and again used to enhance the standing of women, for women, by women, for no other reason than that. This is in the excuse of the lamest kind, to enhance historical female role models, for a modern female society of little substance, in the need of bolstering up, possibly in the guise of encouragement for a higher uptake in the STEM field subjects, of which females seem to avoid. Hedy Lemarr was an extremely sexy and beautiful woman, I could not say as to wether this had a profound bearing on her success, or even the willingness of men allowing her to be part of something she otherwise wouldn't have been a part of, but as with many assumptions the answer is self-evident. On closer inspection of the claim she was co-inventor with a certain Mr George Antheil, the meeting with this man was to enhance her upper body, why this would be so, as he was an accomplished musician is hard to validate, even more bizarre is they got onto the subject of torpedoes, this is a conversation beyond any reasoning, or maybe in that era the first thing one would aspire to is the ability to fully grasp, the workings of The Frequency-Hopping Spread Spectrum Invention, would be an astonishing incite into the social intelligence required at ubiquitous cock tail parties of the day. George, dare I say, would have a direct advantage over Lemarr, as being a pianist, the invention in some way pertained to 88, the amount of keys on the piano, not knowing if Lemarr was also a pianist, I do know her former husband was a munitions manufacture of torpedos.

Maybe this was the inspiration for Lemarr to get the invention of WI-FI of the ground, I suppose her involvement with Howard Hughs, and the streamlining of his aircraft designs, amongst other things, I am sure. With no financial benefit to show, having invented one of the most widely used pieces of technology ion the planet, she must have been in a strong position to claim untold wealth, or is it this persistent ambivalence recording of history once again brought the house of cards crashing down, without so much as a waft from the Argos catalogue.

On watching a television documentary on the great Isambard Kingdom Brunnel, arguably one of, or, indeed the greatest engineer who ever lived, from diversity alone, with such projects as the Great Western Railway, The Clifton Suspension Bridge, along with shipbuilding to name a few, should cement his place in history. With such achievements, the female presenter still felt it necessary to claim, "he was a difficult man to look after", why, according to the eminent female historian, due to excessive cigar smoking, he always had cigar ash down his clothes. Now in an era without washing machines, I have the upmost sympathy for the gigantic task this must have created, for the house maids of the time, but this shallow comment of ridiculous banality is indicative of the female psyche.

Stereotyping was once a a simple matter of common sense, men did the heavy work, women did the light work, due to the obvious difference in physical strength, women had babies, men went to work to support the family, for the simple reason, men cannot bare children. Quite easy so far, is stereotyping bad, it has been around for ever, "horses for courses" or "pigeon holing", all innocent terms, and innocent observations that some people do somethings, and others do other things, that was before the liberal elite high jacked the whole agenda. The way of defining one another, without prejudice to stigma, was whipped up into a frenzy of do's and dont's, can and cant's, mainly for the inclusion of women, all this has nothing to do with stereotyping, but all to do with the misguided thought, that everything men do, women want to do, but are not allowed, due the fact, they are women. On any random selection of a stereotyping example, not to far into the conversation, it becomes a female issue, in all but name of course. On researching the female dilemma, if it exists, marital rape was alluded to, to include this in a piece on stereotyping was a complete cop out, and nothing other than an early chance to get stuck into the male, how sad an interesting subject has to be used in this manner, a damning accusation, to set the ball rolling, and gain sympathy vote from the off. The ends of which are incalculable, that women will go to hear the sound of their own drum, with absolutely no constructive value, whatsoever, and causing the derision they so crave, for the justification of enduring persecution they have withstood since the good lord adorned them with a fanny.

The Establishment of the Working Group by the Human Rights Council Pioneering the Discrimination and Stereotyping Against Women and Their Inclusion in Decision Making. The very wording is a plethora of platitudes to bamboozle and alienate any one reading this title with an ounce of credibility or belief, half way through the nonsense of this title. Who are these feckless, belligerent wannabes, and how are they getting away with endless guff, and regurgitation of facts, that were old hat in Germane Grears day, this endless recycling of non- existent taboos and misdemeanours of centuries gone by are wearing a little thin, to say they are overstated, is in it's self, highly overstated. These Autocrats elevated by no one other than them selves, in a premises of curing all evil, are so detached from the subject, they feel it is their sole purpose in life to redress the non existent imbalance, using tax payers money, for idle chit-chat in coffee bars, on extended lunch breaks, in non-jobs, with full sick pay, holiday pay, and pensions beyond most, these positions held mostly by women, (how could a man understand) are nothing short of an appeasement exercise bye the state.

The stereotyping is over used in the case of employment, to say women are employed in unskilled jobs more than men, maybe true, but the question is why, women choose less lucrative employment, as in part-time, jobs with little or no responsibility or accountability, on the other side of the argument, the man needs to extend himself more, due to in almost all cases being the main breadwinner, a stereotype women now choose to ignore. The stereotype of the grimy, tired workers of the industrial revolution have been shelved, the black faces of the coalminers are being carefully airbrushed out of history, these men drove this country to a pinnacle of success we all now enjoy, non of this is now front page news, a sad indictment to these hard working moral men, to whom any woman could only dream of emulating on such a grand scale.

How would the west have been won, if not for the stereotypical cowboys, another positive view of men to be consigned to the history books on the highest shelf, the cowboys herding cattle across endless dusty plains, whooping and hollering, lasso in one hand six shooter in the other, rough shaven and hard liquor on their breath, a stereotype of a man in a historical reference correct to those times. Does this need airbrushing to include women who could not have survived these difficult work conditions, just imagine women only camp fires (if they could actually light it) bemoaning the men get more money and have the best horses, this of course never happened, because as always women have the luxury to cherry pick in most areas of life. Saloon work was more to the women's liking, out of the elements and comfortable bed, and sharing it for money not a problem, were they trafficked or coerced into this age old profession, maybe, but not many swopped it for the saddle, was it "Annie get your gun" or "Fannie get your douche bag".

We can all recall the black and white poster of the hunky guy with the small baby, another stereotype that became iconic, due to the fact women wanted it to be, wether they wanted a hunk like that of there own, or just the old man to do some babysitting, your guess is as good as mine, the reason this image was so successful, was the opposite, in reality women hold the baby. Trying to enforce stereotypes, or positive profiling I suppose it would be known as, is a bigger waste of time and money it ever was, why are women portrayed in posters in the construction industry with trowels in hand, holding it like a baby holds a fork when learning to eat, this poster girl has and never be the norm the establishment so painfully want it to be. Why is it wrong to portray women as mums (true), and correct to wrongly portray women's involvement in the construction industry (untrue), it is just another fake campaign to enhance the inclusion of women, into some thing they have no interest in, just incase the inequality police get wind of not enough is being done, to promote the un-promotable.

Another body of the nothing else better to do intelligentsia are, The United Nations System-Wide Action Plan on Gender Equality and the Empowerment of Women (UN-SWAP) tactfully abbreviated in their sole aim to SWAP every man's input or influence in the modern world, another divisive and cynical minded, unelected body of sexist thugs, hell bent on creating an uneven playing field, at all costs, for the advancement of the notion of a totalitarian all women state control. To empower is by definition to invest with legal power to authorise this sorry state of delusion, on the behalf of people who are incapable, mentally and physically of performing work that is usually performed by men. The main problem with these beady eyed crackpots, is the quest for the Holy Grail of equality cannot and will not be obtained by misappropriation. In an article by The Daily Telegraph (11/9/19) Ruth Cairnie describes the UK's defence industry as one of the strongest and internationally competitive industries the UK has recently championed, then in the same article, to a meddlesome rhetoric that the launch of The Women in Defence Charter, is much needed, in order I suppose, to again remove men of senior positions to favour women, men who by Cairnie's own admission are doing a great job, all in the name of gender diversity. To fudge, force and blur at every chance, the woman's view in whatever they feel it should be, as for the undeserved enhancement of female careers to the detriment of men, solely in the name of diversification is ludicrous and unfounded, these desperate measures to interfere in an already highly successful industry, shows how desperate woman are to be involved in an already well run and respected set up, with tweaking and underhand introduction of legislation, for them to take on positions way beyond their acumen, can only have a negative impact.

In technology and science alongside inventors, woman still lag way behind, even with all the positive discrimination they receive, by all the bodies of people well salaried at the tax payers cost, to discriminate and blame men for all women's shortfalls and lack of inclusion, in only the things of course they wish to be included. Women's own ineptitude to carry out work and sheer lack of of desire to succeed in anything that requires a certain level of commitment is there for all to see, but the blame is not all there's, due to always having a fiscal safety net in place, be it a man or the state, the propensity to give up on something remotely out of their comfort zone is surely, partly due to this.

In the history of art the contribution of women is a rarity, and is almost completely dominated by men, it is not merely a coincidence, more a case of male perception alongside the ability to turn existential themes into believable works that command recognition and admiration with the appreciation of beauty without jealousy, a depth of integrity in paintings or sculptures, and many other genres, that the females seem to lack. A case of physicality may come into question in the brutal chipping away at rock for months on end in the art of sculpture, may have been to much for wrists used to washing clothes and peeling the veg, this is not coincidence merely evolution. How did the cave-people evolve with out equality, and rafts of laws and regulations to enhance women's rights, how did they survive with the thought that one was suitable for certain jobs, which others were not, the delegation was of pure basic cerebella intuition, that in modern times, the thought is to include all (women) at the cost of all others (men) is sadly lost.

If you take the patrons of the Moulin Rouge which opened in 1889, Toulouse Latrec being one of many famous men to frequent this den of budding artists, living in squalor and combined with hard liquor and much more, these men impressed the world with their talent, the public were intrigued and rhapsodised them for their brilliance. The main contribution by women was to dance The Can Can with the modesty of underwear, not adhered to, a sight I feel well worth a look, as the dance drew to a close, hiding behind numerous Ostrich feathers, the women then sold to the highest bidder, the very item that was earlier on show. Commendable I am sure, maybe being born with with an inbuilt prized commodity, is such a game changer, that the art of painting etc is not an option, due to the ease this biological goldmine can be employed with little or no talent or gruelling suffrage of training. So basically, laying on ones back for ten minutes, to ensure your day to day needs are met, is unlike Michelangelo's laying on his back for four years to do the same, the disparity is clear of what men will endure, more than women, to achieve not only notoriety, but a desire to attain respect in their chosen field.

All the female talent of present and historical times, surely cannot have been suppressed through domestic commitments that has been suggested, this has to be seen as nonsense, even to the lay-man or lay-women, or indeed the lay-person, with even a pea sized brain to hand.

The Unmade Bed, by Tracey Emin, sperm soaked and condom strewn, is hardly, Henry Moore or Constable, but as in all things blurred lines and the quest to innovate and desecrate any formula, that woman find hard to aspire to or on any reasonable terms never achieve. The exquisite levels of profound beauty and brilliance attained again and again by men, has to be called into question for no other reason than female contributions are inadequate in most fields dominated by men. As hard as it is to swallow, swallow is a must or the questions will never be answered, only the worthless rigmarole of hand wringing and why is it so, and when the questions are all exhausted, lets just except, men are mostly better at all guises of art than women. Singing is different as it is a natural gift, which needs little work to perfect, women are on par with men in this field. Then there is the so called genre of literature called "chick lit" as the name suggests is written predominantly for women, thus the contents are below par and lacking any true literal geniuses with in it's ranks. The likes of Fifty Shades of Grey a tome mainly purchased by sexless, women of a certain age, and I suggest that a large percentage of the book was either never read, or left in a 3 star hotel room in Benidorm, with the top corner of page 12 folded.

The other copies lapped up with vigour (a spike in sales of butt plugs to the over fifties) causing mayhem in the sanctuary of inactivity of the bedroom, now long forgotten demands reappear, for the re-enactment of not only the past, but also what is with in the pages of FSofG. I am sure this has ruined many a Saturday evening with the stand off, of delaying retiring to the once pleasant and comfortable slumberland by watching television late into the night, in order not to wake his partner, and keep Pandora's box under the bed firmly closed. With sacred heroines such as Bridget Jones, seen as icons of the female form and champions of all manner of somewhat difficult circumstances (usually of their own making), gives a president to believe without question that all other women can overcome what ever situation they choose, with white wine, food, friends and a lot of crying, this encourage young girls into a falsehood of impunity, at the cost of a fair society. Now, Chick Lit has been acclaimed and honoured and created a swimming pool full of money for the mainly female authors and publishers, shit sells as always, that's fine but trying to justify this as having any literary substance, because of sales, is akin to saying Macdonalds are the finest restaurants. The great Doris Lessing said of Chick Lit, " it is instantly forgettable".

CHAPTER SIX

Pornography and prostitution are the mainstays of many men's sex lives, although this being a taboo matter, it is never the less true, due to complete lack of sexual, and even any physical contact in the stale event of being with a partner for to long, this occurs for many reasons.

Complacency and familiarity are two, also after childbirth, and the big slimming exercise for the wedding day photos, goes into reverse, in both cases the pounds pile on, "I am comfortable and there is more of me to love" is just an example of the pathetic rhetoric, spewed out by idle females, 7,8,9 dress sizes bigger, the husband, "I like my women with a bit of meat on them", if so why do they cease to fuck them any more, afraid to mention the elephant in the room, hooked on daytime television and part-time work, if any. I am not a doctor, but logic tells me there is no need to pile on six stones, to give birth to something that weighs seven pounds, I am aware of the extra fluids needed for the babies survival, but the childish "I am eating for two", two of what, I find it hard to believe that a foetus has had time to develop a penchant for Macdonalds and Ben and Jerries, washed down with gallons of diet coke, diet in the coke being the only saving grace. The lack of sexual desire, decreases slowly, until it becomes the Saturday bath night special, or birthdays, or maybe she needs a new coat, all the controlling of this aspect of marriage soon turns the man completely off, having to fight for sex, is demeaning, and the whole moment of "oh! Go on then hurry up" is lost, and sometimes never found.

The myth that coercion, is the reason most women turn to prostitution or pornography as a career is from the mouths of haggard feminists and men who watch baking programmes, yes it does happen, but these very well paid women who have made huge sums out of the sex industry, only become victims when it suits them, usually when they have been operating covertly and get found out. The woman knows no depths as to which to plummet in the quest for financial reward, having every orifice stretched by huge male members, with a look of ecstasy on her you innocent face, is almost hard to watch. As prostitution and pornography flourish, the main benefactors being women, and as usual the the financial burden is with the man, in the twisted one sided debate the decision to try to demonise the one buying and not the one selling is ludicrous, imagine applying this to the drug trade, but then again if all dealers were women I suppose that would be ok. The main protest comes from women who have frankly had their day, and even in their prime, could not have cut it in either industry. Even stranger, these sabre rattling hypocritical self-serving breed of feminists, who by the way will rally to any backwater cause, from free tampons to the enforced wearing of miniskirts and high heels for women who want to look and feel sexy, are trying their upmost to put their sisters out of work, and will blame men for this catastrophe of modern times of exploitation and human slavery and trafficking, with out the thought to speak to the women they are trying to save. I am in no way trying to confuse the high end of prostitution with the low end of the market, in all jobs there are discrepancies, in wages, the better you portray yourself in any type of employment, the more you earn, and to what level you wish to aspire to is also an important factor.

Men have prostituted their bodies for centuries in war, mining, and construction just to name a few, enduring savage injuries, death and debilitating illnesses of which end in a slow excruciating death, women rarely have to have to suffer any of this, in order to save ones liberty, or put food on the table. Prostitution and pornography can be given up at any time, almost without risk to ones health, all sexual diseases can be cured, and with safe practice not even contracted. The mental side, to these occupations are no worse than the things life will throw at you, divorce, death of loved ones, etc. People, who try to justify or excuse the reasons for these women's actions, usually ones who have never been directly involved, site drug use, economic issues. What is the difference to a man working on a construction site to fund his habit (the main difference it will take him all day to earn what she gets in an hour). Sometimes when things are simplified for all to understand, the point would be met easily, that is why so called academics like to cloak these activities in sociology and psychology and a plethora of other ologies to justify their unnecessary complex, well funded studies. In most cases the sex industries are on a sound footing, but like any industry with a vast amount of employees, pitfalls and collateral damage will occur, to elevate the sex industry to a higher level than others is deeply flawed. The notion that all women are some how forced into the sex industries has to be addressed, if these industries are so dangerous and demeaning, why is the uptake of positions sky rocketing, easy money is the only answer. One hundred and thirty pounds an hour, and up to one thousand pounds is achievable, where could any normal person (because that's what these women are) expect such a wonderful return on their endeavours, we all know the answer to that.

Pornography once the preserve of the wealthy, (like most things) with grainy black and white images of victorian ladies, and slide shows eagerly waited for men of the day adorned in velvet gold piped smoking jackets, is now an industry of huge magnitude, and unlimited access to all.

Genres, some prior to this huge success never even heard of, magazines then videos then cds, now multi media phones, porn on the go, porn everywhere. We are constantly bashed over the head by the idea it is corrupting young boys into thinking it is normal to have sex with beautiful slim girls, a sad shout out to all those Biffas moaning, it is normal. It can improve ones knowledge and techniques, but as always women have to play the victim card, it encourages boys to mistreat girls, maybe the girls earning all the money from this should make more love friendly movies, and perhaps marry the male lead at the end, oh please. Through the ages good and bad have co- existed, and it is ones personal duty to be responsible for their actions or indeed non-action, if you do not want pictures of your genitals shared anywhere else other than with the person you want to, it's easy, do not take pictures of them, let alone send them to someone you have just met. There I assume are many fake agencies, but on answering an advert to model swimwear, a harmless photo shoot agreed before one would even show up, with the idea these women have that they are catwalk standard, just shows the self-importance felt with in ordinary women, fed by constant mantras of the modern era, to end up getting fucked by two guys, it is hard to understand how one thing led to another, and she had no idea or choice in how this situation manifested itself into a fantastic earning opportunity, onward and upward.

It is said only humans and dolphins have sex for pleasure only, there has since time began a human fascination with sex, to try to departmentalise this with whys and therefores, and try to blame on any one thing why sex is so important (some of us) even if we don't do it we talk about it, men more than women, I think not, women are more secretive about all aspects of sex, a woman being deflowered by just anybody is not a good vibe, but by a legitimate suitor that's fine.

As many women watch porn as men, this is not freely discussed due to the stigma loaded upon the industry, which men find less of a problem. As the woman has the bit of kit between her legs to nullify any failings she may have, overweight, not pretty or just a nasty person, the tool of manipulation can be deployed at any time or circumstance, an asset without any contenders and truly god given. This is why the noble art of prostitution has stood the test of time in all it's guises throughout, history and all cultures, Mary Magdelen a prominent exponent it is thought. The lure of a a sexual encounter is of mind bending proportions that women have profited from it from day one. With house work being claimed as unpaid work, how long before the opening of the legs on Saturday after the ten o'clock news becomes another domestic financial issue, and if he don't fancy it will a rebate be applied.

The females will to deceive is never more evident in their appearance, or the disguise of their true appearance, with endless items, push up bras and girdles and of course face creams gleaned from the inner ear of the rare Pigmy Kingfisher of Borneo. The myriad of disguises are only revealed during the coming together in the bedroom, where the state of undress is unavoidable, in this shocking event on the removal of the weapons of mass deception, the gut will heave, the tits will sag and the make up deposited on the pillow case, a morning leg over may occur if levels of alcohol are still high enough, but as for further meetings in the future, the man is already wracking his brain in order to deflect any incoming suggestions. When the alcohol recedes and the complimentary cup of coffee has been drank, she begins to come to terms with the fact that she has been breeched, which in her mind warrants some idle chatter and at the very least a fictitious dinner date mulled over. The sex has happened, her cards all played, she's played her trump card in the first hand, phone numbers exchanged, dates set never to be honoured, towards the end of the path she looks back, the door is already shut, then she starts the walk of shame.

This journey is usually taken on a Sunday morning before the pubs open, skirt to short for this time of day, high heels, a friend is notified and comes to the rescue, on picking her up, the question is "was he any good" "will you see him again", on the coldness of the breakfast experience still fresh in her mind, she announces "he was shit in bed" and "a pencil dick" the desire not to see him again, has to be shown, to have been her choice and hers alone.

With all the so called advancements that are claimed to be made, mostly for the benefit of women, how come sex is still as taboo as it was in the 1940s. Innocent television ads, laughing at under wear blown off the line, found by an elderly lady next door, on returning it over the fence, the younger lady fakes embarrassment, is it due to the size, as the younger lady matures, so will her underwear, from nice half cheek numbers, to the apple catchers the old lady sports at present, or is there more to it than that. Is the embarrassment shown because of what goes in the knickers, what happens when the knickers are removed, in any other reason than using the toilet, this childish interaction between two adult women epitomises the unease we still choose to surround any thing remotely to do with sex. These draconian actions and every snigger behind the hand, is all to enhance the value of pussy, a less obtainable commodity is desired more and if it can be shrouded in mystery that's even better. After all for most women this prized asset is all they will have to bargain with through out their lives, so it is understandable they don't want to give it away on the cheap. So when the age is right sex is deemed a bad thing, well sort of, it is more a case to whom they give it to, and is it there benefit to allow such a coming together, is there any long term financial gain etc.

All the porn in the world unfortunately, will never substitute the real thing, all the movies made, the easy money made, the fame and all that goes with it, every movie ends, more or less the same. Most women claim not to like or even watch porn, the problem with porn for women is it devalues their own pussy, a man can switch on at any time, to an array of naked beauties, much better than the one he has access to, unless he is extremely lucky, or of course rich, but you can't touch it, thats true, but you don't have to talk to it either, or take it out for a meal before or after, and when you have done, switch here off and go and clean the car. Women have used sex as a way to gain advantage over men throughout history, with all the female bluster and denials they are always the key holder to the main event. With all their adornments in place and a certain knowingness, they move in circles that will bare the best fruit, be it a bar or office, the contact with the right men is essential. The attraction has to be announced, and the announcement acknowledged and suitably received, this ridiculous mantra women 'want an alpha male to protect them, kill wild beasts to feed the kids, this goes back to a time before hot water, houses, cars and financial fortunes, and marriage and of course the divorce lawyers. To be a creature in demand the modern man must be of substance (money) and show prospects, even if he has none, as a ride on the shirt tails can be a bumpy one, so the destination must be of worth to her. He must be strong in the boardroom, but weak in the living room, a willingness to take blame at all times, to take all responsibility when things go wrong, no praise when they don't. Physicality has been taken over by fiscallity, and the women really don't care where the money comes from, after all they know a fraud or cheat will all ways get by, only the straight man bares the brunt when the bad times come knocking.

Sex has been the main lever in life almost exclusively used by women, to steal from men, wealth, property and in many cases their sanity. When certain historical figures such as Casonova was to have hundreds of women free, due, allegedly to the size of his penis, was at the time a celebrity and man of standing in the community, mainly down to his sexual prowess, respected by men and woman. Of course in these times he would have been seen as an irresponsible idiot, duping poor unsuspecting women into sex, a monster. All said and done the very mention of big dick, for all the female chagrin, will keep them coming. The same cannot be said for Cleopatra, used her charms to obtain power, wealth and control and seen as an icon and role model. With most woman sex and love go hand in hand, sex is a physical act, love an emotional act, so in this they are very different, so I find it odd that love has to be the remit to give the pussy a work out, or maybe an excuse for giving it away cheaply. These unwritten moral codes such as these are put in place to excuse the act of fucking as if it was a bad pastime, if there was no personal gain. The women are made to feel stupid and aggrieved at allowing a man to enjoy her sacred rose with out concrete evidence that this act will some how enhance her being, wether it be money or love, of which both are as destructive as the other, why not enjoy the experience of sex without expectations or conditions, the reason we cannot, woman have this free at source.

The one night stand is a coming together of two consenting adults, mostly after alcohol consumption, the man no problem, the woman no problem at the time, I have yet to see a happy female drunk, who by the end of the evening has not started crying and then pissed herself. Same as the smoking of roll ups and drinking pints, females are desperate to buy into all and every pursuit that is male, most of all they fall embarrassingly short, football, cricket and the one night stand. After a night of sucking and licking, gyrating and frenzied orgasms and the swapping of personal body fluids, if the outcome is not to the female liking, it must have been a "misunderstanding" or he is a "user", a man would never claim this after a spontaneous dalliance, because the man understands the basic dynamic, it's a "one night stand". The upsetting thing for the woman is the lack of build up to the event, the build up is paramount, cocktails and an expensive meal sets a more acceptable reason to disrobe on the first date without shame, picked up in a nice car and fucked in a nice bed, surrounded by nice things, means prospects she could well get used to. Over dinner the babbling brook of bollocks slips over smooth pebbles with ease the banality of ten year olds, polarised thoughts, neither care much, he wants what is in those new lacy knickers, she's happy to be seen with well groomed respectable suitor, financially sound, a male other females would be jealous of a man others would covert (days gone by he would have been described as her fancy man), she will inevitably be looking further into the future than he. If she feels the scenario is to her liking, sex on the first night is viewed as collateral damage. On the usual alcohol fuelled one night stand nothing has been discussed, not that either party can remember, when she reunites her dirty knickers with her arse the gloom descends, the hope of another coming together somewhat remote, and who will find out, or simple lies "nothing happened" "

I slept in the spare room, and he brought me breakfast in bed, a real gentleman" highly unlikely, as we all know, friends ask will you see him again, he's not my type she muses, all this running through her mind at speed sitting on the edge of his bed with a hangover, how will i get home, who will I call. As she sits on the bed head in hands bent forward, she can smell her pussy, her mind wanders were only a women's can.

The man is fine with the one night stand, because in general he is ok about sex, doesn't get to hung up about it, other than there is not enough of it, and do not over think or over state it's value, unlike women, who feel there must be a reason for it. If a woman puts it about a bit, and is a little carefree, other woman see her as the enemy, not to be trusted around their men whom they have under firm control, but worst of all it devalues their prize asset, and with it being given away unconditionally, makes the other women outdated and redundant. For what ever reason some women do not put it about or are unable to, be it jealousy, or over valuing what they have or giving it no value at all, it doesn't stop them name calling (slut) or being unfair and very wary of the more liberal of the gender.

The very idea of sex within marriage is belittled and the butt of many jokes, but the theme is always the same, she has it, he wants it, and the whole marriage can be controlled by her with out question. Sex becomes treated by her as just another household chore, means to an end, this debasement of the very thing she held in such high esteem is way to demonise sex, to use it in many guises to the woman's advantage, birthday blow jobs, not yours, her's, in order to maximise any spending that may occur, it makes a mockery of the first thing that attracted us to one another. It is also another way to keep up the taboo, the man desiring something out of bounds, until she deems it a necessary. In a manner that can only be described unhealthy, this clandestine treatment of such a natural action becomes more and more of an issue, made out be a male deficiency of want, is another way to bump up the value and control, and in the end sex is no talked about, never mind performed, a dead pool of silence engulfs any couple of a certain age, who should still be enjoying sex, at the diner table when the subject is aroused.

Flirting for drinks not far from soliciting for money is inexcusable, it would not be permitted in any other circumstance, imagine a woman making idle conversation in the butchers in order to get the man to pay for her sausages, the difference in venue should not make it correct, this type of behaviour should be seen for what it is fraud and deception leading to entrapment, as with the wolf whistle from thirty feet in the air, this female premeditated behaviour should be punishable by law. Easily dismissed as harmless fun (by women) but the sums of money involved otherwise suggest other, up ward of thirty pounds for a round of drinks in a night club, purchased by a victim hardly rolling in money, thinking naively it's the company she wants " a fool and his (not her) his money are easily parted" what a horribly cynical tern of phrase, so the men are fools, and in some twisted way it's their fault for being generous and trusting at face value, the world would be a baron place without interaction and even better with more honesty. He will go home broke, she will bump into other men, more drinks, she will go home with a full purse, she may even get pissed and enter the world of one night stands, and the user will get used, this would be such an apt and fitting end to the evening.

After all the whys and where for the question will never be answered, why do we become so obsessed about sex, even before we have taken part, yes it can be nice and sometimes amazing but so can a good meal, the next day the meal is forgotten but sex is still top of the menu. You may feel the meal is not so important, if you don't eat you die, if you don't fuck you still live. It can not be from childhood that we are conditioned to want sex, because rightly so the topic is not suitable for the very young. When of certain age we start to become aware of sex and see it's presence in everyday life, then the parents begin the difficult task to make teenagers aware of dangers and badness of sex, almost always from the mother, keep the pussy locked away the value from an early age engrained into the girls psyche, keep away from them boys, they are only after one thing, and so on, the seen is set in realm of sex, the girls have it the boys want it. The losing of a boys virginity is seen to be a normal occurrence on the path to manhood, with the girls this is quite a different matter, it is a thing to be held onto at all costs for as long as possible, with divisive language such as " she lost her virginity" "she gave it away to soon", is just another way of demonising the act and the man involved, from the off sex is seen as a male issue or a female issue, never a combined issue, and always the man is portrayed as the aggressor, and until this is addressed, the first time for many will be a catastrophe, down to the ignorance of the ones who should know better.

Dating sites are the new phenomenon, this form of matchmaking is ideal for women, the lies and false claims are reeled off behind a screen, the secret chubbsters munching away on crisps and chocolate bars washed down with diet coke, lying about every thing in a hope of getting a seat at the table of life, if when out and about and viewed in the flesh they would find it much harder to achieve this. It is a pretty slim chance that you can explain away the ageing of ten years and the gaining of five stone in two days, and they won't even try. The woman's view is the very thing they despise, the need for the male to be chivalrous, in order not to offend, and 99 times out of 100 will be polite and still pay for dinner. The men very rarely complain and on recounting the experiences find humour is the best answer, a lot of men are desperate to be in the game of relationships, to be included in this fantasy world of nonsense, or just plain desperate, desperation is a great leveller, and easy to exploit, men do not expect Demi Moore, but a woman who's thigh (yes, one of them) is equivalent to his waist, and a head like a 30 bob cabbage is a little to much deception to handle in one go. Average body type, that is the female claim, well I assume they are unaware of the meaning of both average and type, there is nothing average at 5 feet tall and coming in at 15 stone, maybe average in her circle of associates, but never average elsewhere. The classroom clown is another generic term used, this conjures up to me, her being a twat after a few drinks. Men are not looking for love, neither are most women, that's why the man rolls over and pays for dinner, sex is what is sought after, the men freely admit this, but as usual the woman has to romanticise the whole event in order to give away the jewel in their crown. For the men it's a bet on an old nag some you win some you lose, the excitement is in the race, and with some you end up tightening the odd bolt or two. The waitress is usually more interesting than the dinner date, having seen it many times, reading the man's expression on first sight, and exchanging a wry smile before approaching the table, a hidden theme develops throughout the evening between the man and the waitress, a subtle admission of being duped, acknowledged.

Nevertheless the woman plods on with her invisible rhetoric, between huge mouthfuls of food, the tragedy within him is raw, she, enthralled in her own brilliance, doesn't even notice no one is listening. As in all things her problems are everyones problems, the man's problems are his, and he should man up and do something about it. After all the promises to keep in touch, she knows this is never going to happen, so does he, a civil way to end an evening built on lies that it should end on one too.

With our never ending quest for love if is easy to immortalise and fantasise, but in most men's head it's just an act of self-indulgence and pretence, as long as she can cook and knows the way around the bedroom that's fine. With her love is the expensive wedding, the 5000 pound honeymoon, the new house, it's all material, then love has no intellectual value or it wouldn't exist, love can mean so many things, to no one.

In the American civil war as usual the sex industry was swept under the carpet, it was rife and pretty damn ripe to I would wager, air brushed out of history, again for the women's protection.

The world must respect the prostitutes, no matter how false the portrayal, history is massaged into anything other than the truth, all ways to save the denigration of the female form, even with no schooling they used what was available, what was in their knickers, as soon as they realised the knickers were worth more down than up. A certain Joseph Hooker took the matter to task, hence the name "hookers" was born and used ever since. Men everywhere, death everywhere, alcohol everywhere, women everywhere, the scene is set for a sex sale bonanza, the woman predated on these men for financial gain, not to put food on the table for the kids (that old chestnut) or any other reason other than greed. With upwards of 100,000 men in the field, it was like shooting fish in a barrel, the fanny rolled in and the foreskins rolled back, fanny again at a premium, highly overvalued easy money, the men thinking this might be the last chance to indulge or even the first time, the female ideology is trashed at the notion of coercion or pimps duping innocent young girls, most of these prostitutes travelled alone of their own accord, following the tales of the riches to be had. There was a serious down side to this, the detriment of the soldiers thus the army, more men syphed up in hospital than men with battle field injuries, the forces were being decimated by these diseased ridden screwballs, so something had to change. Sex it's self was not the problem, but the way it was used, the business model had not been thought out correctly, sheer numbers and poor hygiene led to the problem. It is said some women joined the army in the guise of being a man, in order to get a more exclusive pick of work, by being under the radar at surrounded with cock, (a gallant notion, there was probably six who went to such lengths) this determination to get ahead in ones business is nevertheless quite impressive, are they to be heralded every where, statues erected in public places to emphasise the huge commitment and ingenuity these women have shown in order to champion ones self in an extremely difficult and competitive market, and then hold role model status (come on Brittany, if they could make it there, surly you can make it here). 48 % of the soldiers had a sexual transmitted disease, the women kept coming, with easy money to be made it was hopeless, until the clinics were set up, fannies checked 5 dollars a go, the whole business was legalised.

As soon as word got out about the existence of the clinic, even more hookers turned up, no room for the timid, this was now hard nosed business, professionals the only survivors.

Much of the correspondence the soldiers sent home was to be vetted and altered if any mention of the hookers was present. Just in case any of the hookers named were recognised on return back home and ostracised and rendered unmarryable, the cover up was on, in the context of the brutality of the war and millions of casualties, why the insistence of this cosmetic exercise, again the mind boggles at the sensitivity woman have to be shown even in the event of committed shameful acts.

One of the reasons women do not like prostitutes, they say, is it gives the sisters a bad name, well, I think that's not it at all, the prostitutes allow men to buy sex at cost, and unlike many wives' the prostitutes make an effort, it's their chosen field and if you want repeat clients in any business, all needs must be met with a polite and helpful manner. The other huge plus is you get sex with out the 30 sentence of marriage. Stunning beauty or in most cases just a hint of it, in the selfie obsessed vacant modern day females, breeds horrible traits in these wannabes, arrogance and self worth are just two, two paces behind the gym addicted bull follows, this existence devoid of any intellect or desire to educate ones self, the expectation of a smooth passage through life because of who these young women think they are, the destination is usually failure, due to lack of effort and ambition, when the going gets tough they get gone. With age the beauty becomes a tool that can no longer be utilised, this is certainly the bitterest pill to swallow, 30 years on, the men are not looking anymore, with the lust and wish to bed this wonderful creature, all that once was just a matter of being has now changed, every thing obtained in the past with minimum effort (obviously, if to much effort was required they would not bother) a flick of the hair, a shake of the ass or a coy smile, used to do the trick, the demise must be crushing, with age they become invisible, now in the man's world, if they want something, from now on they must earn it. Whilst watching there nemesis's reeled off the conveyor belt of life, having nightmares in their sertraline dreams of young beautiful women, with bodies sealing the deals they once could, now mothers instead of being daughters, time always has the last laugh. Many women become train wrecks searching in the tangled mess they have created, looking for answers to their own problems. If they do not make plenty of hay when the sun shines, before they know it the barn will be empty.

Old pussies depreciate quicker than new cars, becoming after a short period of time virtually worthless, the shit storms the woman could cause in days gone by, is just now a distant memory, if the profit is not made early in years the game is up, all of the fights, all the heartache inflicted on men in this catch me if you can behaviour, is diminished by the years rolling on. This once five star all-inclusive attraction, has become a self catering minus the towels and bedding. The mire deepens with the onset of the menopause, the once scenic lush lady garden, has now dried up, the only curtains regularly open and closed, are the ones purchased at B and M, the beef variety long since removed from the menu. Even the modern postage stamp no longer requires a licking.

CHAPTER SEVEN

The soap opera has long been a yard stick over the years as a dynamic to judge the female metronome of absolute ridiculousness, beyond comprehension, alongside reality television which is self serving plethora of excuses, why it is not their fault, and why they are at the bottom of the pile of life, with the haggard and less haggard, bouncing from one "unavoidable" society driven crisis to another, with a notion everything is out of their control. Relationships within relationships with out guilt, until discovery occurs, then the generic mantra floods out, lack of attention and lack of understanding, being two of the usual suspects that forced her to drop the knickers in the search for a soulmate and a friend, "someone she could talk to", I could go on, but I won't. The man's take on it is much simpler, he wants beauty and sexual excitement, be it the girl in the cafe or the cleaner at work, social and financial standings are irrelevant. The woman's agenda is to be seen to be bettering herself (not hard in most cases) at someone else expense and vainly feel something good transpire, most men see this as the dead duck it is. The pairing of a female doctor with a postman, or any other manual worker, unless this is during training, before she transcends into the beautiful butterfly of a qualified clinician, then in most cases as in the police force, the old man is redundant and the consultant or chief inspector become the new target.

Once the man's objective has been reached and the underwear

breeched, the interest is quickly lost, unless the experience is of mind-blowing proportions, or some thing very different, once, all has been revealed, the man feels mission accomplished, all the small talk, said, but women have a great deal of trouble dealing with this, so the man most pay for stepping outside the lines she has subconsciously drawn. If he is married, all of which she was aware of, the start of the nightmare begins, the wish to destroy all before her is common, where as when a man becomes surplus to requirements he will rarely destroy something that from the start was not his, just for the sake of it. The woman however see this a direct insult and slap in the face, once the holy grail has been deployed (the minge) it is her and only her who will finish the affair, again it comes down to full control of the situation, if this control is overlooked, she will destroy everything, even her own life, careers and families are meaningless, once she embarks on this crusade in the name being used and disrespected, any type of carnage is justified.

The soap opera is the perfect platform for these female grievances against men, these high powered machiavellian matriarchs ensconced in their kingdoms, hoovering up everyones emotions and family problems to add to their own, with the flick of the hairbrush and a strong pull on a mayfair smooth. Of course she presides over all before her, in the council house kangaroo court, solving problems, of their own making, and at the same time creating many more, with their war babies scattered all around and the single mum carer playing at the very lives they watch religiously week in week out with the morbid hope that the next episode will be more gruesome and profoundly sad than the last, and watch it all again on a lazy Sunday in their onesies. Nothing better than an errant child turning up, to tighten an already sagging story line, a product of a brief affair some twenty years ago, to spark up the dull proceedings the relevant husband has to except this, due to the time passed, and anyway we are not real men if we are unable or god forbid, unwilling, to absorb such matters, the real issue is the sexual desire for the perpetrator, has all but gone, so the thought of her with another man has little baring on the husbands emotions.

As in all walks of life, a successful man is always suspect, and in a perverse way be found out at all costs. Mike Baldwin in the soap opera Coronation Street, was a prime example, he owned the factory and employed the very women who threw themselves at him, these women at the same time despised him, because of his Jaguar car and scotch in the Rovers Return public house instead of a pint of beer. Always cast as a villain, yet he brought employment and wages into homes, this all may sound trivial, but the devotees who lap up every word, and repeat and discuss these fictitious characters and events, as if they are real. The soap opera portrays itself as a barometer of real life, which it is not, it panders to to women with its facile and unflinching view of normality. Another such series, Emerdale, with the Farm now removed of course, was once a pleasant drama in the green fields of Yorkshire, with Annie Sugden being the matriarch, a dour and unhappy soul, and Seth being the exception, an affable poacher, maybe a story was missed there. Now to the present day, with its B-lister painted ladies, with the acting skill of a scarecrow, which in some cases the so called actresses would scare the crows in a more convincing manner, tearing up the leafy lanes in their procured Range Rovers, not a hair out of place or a dreaded broken nail to be seen, and the aroma of cow shit just a distant memory, and to even suggest a couple of hours after dark in the lambing shed would be greeted with laughter, whilst quaffing Prosecco in the Woolpak Public house, as these dunderheads chirp away about the next tanning session. Eastenders was at the start the Den and Angie show, husband and wife, him of course being dirty Den, and she a helpless alcoholic, due to Den's unruly behaviour, the die was cast and the sympathy vote Secured. Then there was the Mitchell brothers and Nick Cotton or nasty Nick as he was to become, these men all cast as villainous, whilst on the other side was, Sharon, bar maid/victim and Dot Cotton, mum/victim and so on. Why is the need to demonise men so attractive, it is the need to captivate the audience, which runs into tens of millions every week, of which a very high proportion are women, so to execute and have men hung drawn and quartered in the pursuit of entertainment is acceptable, and if possible, the traits will be reenacted, within the lives of real families. He sits there, drinks a cup of tea he made, dunks the biscuits, he bought, unacknowledged, whilst she is glued to the sad demise of any man in the firing line in the latest instalment. With no empathy, these disgusting scenarios, are gobbled up with out question, due the false portrayal of the quarry, these onesie wearing unemployed pits of humanity, who feel in full command of all around them, soaking up the endless financial support, they feel is owed to them, the determining factor in all this, is simple, they can carry babies, a skill which in a world heading for 7 billion, I find highly overrated. The whole of society hoodwinked the notion that being a woman, and being able to have children is all it requires to be the saviour of mankind, when in the future the child will be gestated in some thing akin to a grow bag, the literal comparison is yours.

CHAPTER EIGHT

A work colleague once explained the scenario of his recent down fall, his wife of many years decided she wanted to break free from the terrible marriage she was in, so the rock solid reasons which are the go to, and can never be questioned, by any one with an ounce of empathy toward mankind, mainly the female mankind of course, were trotted out. The usual story was concocted, one of domestic violence, combined with drunken behaviour, this will give the authorities carte blanche in all matters, no matter if unsubstantiated, the authorities will carry out her desires to destroy and eradicate her once loving husband. After the removal of my colleague from the house he had dutifully secured for his family through all weathers and ups and downs, she installed another man, who now sleeps in the very bed he paid for, and probably on the same side as not to upset her routine, and kisses his children goodnight, all whilst he snuggles up on a mates settee. She kept the car he is still paying for, the mortgage he still pays, most bills, alongside trying to keep his self fed and sane. Having the audacity to by himself a 300 pound car, for visiting and trips out for the kids, after the first visit in the said vehicle, early in the next week a demand arrived at his mates house from her solicitor, for half the value of the vehicle, this brutal hounding and the tearing away of all he once had and loved ended up in a nervous breakdown, all his teeth fell and he now lives in a barge. I would at this point wish to complement all involved in the destruction of this man, in a job executed without mercy or thought, and hope in the very near future a not to dissimilar predicament invades their lives with such force and indignity. Why was all this allowed to happen, it was for the children's benefit and safety, well you may pretend to believe that, the benefit of destroying the children's father has no benefit at all, other than the woman's side of gain and power, the upside the kids will grow up and work it all out and realise what a loud of shit the system is, and then later in life become victims of it, because we never learn.

In the relationship, the constant fight for financial equality is ever present, with hardly ever a financial equality of input, these parasitic mercenary beasts, championed by the state the establishment and rancid liberalism, are on the war path for the equality of every thing for the input of nothing. The support of all things detrimental to the male, to the extent of astounding length of which no effort was made by the woman, but she will reap benefit after reward after benefit for nothing other than whats in her nickers. Screeching disillusionment with the system, which by the way is almost solely run and managed for the preference of woman's failings and lack of ability to attend to their own affairs, absolute lack of control of the basics in life, pointing the finger, and crying betrayal, through the lack of not enough free money being available. If you are a single mother struggling to manage, why would you have another child with a man you have only known for three months, and some warped mindset think it will make things better. We are all aware of the fundamental right to bare children you cannot support, and have no where for them to live, without a shred of responsibility for nothing, not even the human being they force into a society they have no input themselves, on the premiss everything will be alright. History tells us it won't be alright, these women have full control over all the options and with a little moral conscience and a lot less help from the state, they could in some cases arrive at a different outcome, but don't hold your breathe.

Men are extending themselves far to much, with long hours

and responsibilities in a sense of duty to the family, to supply the standard of living modern times seem to require, all of this post marriage support is nothing short of blackmail, strangled by over zealous courtrooms financial demands, and required by the media and all other biased and sexist institutions to be the alpha male, in all but name only of course, alongside responsibility for all things financial. Any financial failure to beset his family will be attributed to his failing, although being evicted from the house he paid for, for the sake of his children, he still wishes to enhance and for fill the future of, the law still deal any blow they care, the financial pressure is colossal, he feels a need to work and take risks to keep everything afloat, and himself too, with a detrimental effect to physical and mental health, the ex-wife remains unmoved by his plight, literally and emotionally, and receives help from every phone line she cares to call, from the comfort of his sofa. All this life long indoctrination by the to do the right thing is aimed at men, even when the children are not theirs they feel obligated to help, be it granddad or brother, how many woman feel the same, a limited number I would say.

Fat mothers, fat kids, it's in the genes, or a malfunction of the glands, I say, it's not the glands but the hands, and what the hands put into the mouth, the feeding of young children is almost exclusively in control of the mothers, this choice of allowing the child abuse of their own children by not controlling diets, will fail these children, into a life of ill health, due to the lazy and ignorant behaviour of those they look up to and should who have the best interest for them, alas in to many cases this is not so.

A fatherless child will as all data suggests fail, no matter what chaotic circumstance the child is born, the errant father or the state will pay and will continue to pay for all mental health issues and crimes committed by these children, all of this is well documented and known to be so. So these women fed on a diet of self-gratification in all areas of society that no financial repayment will be required from them for their part in the implosion of modern society. The stabbings of young men, drug related gang affiliation, almost all off this is due to a lack of fatherhood or presence of any men involved in the child's upbringing. So the question that is never asked is why are these women having babies sometimes multiple babies with the same man or different men who they now have never and will never help them. Surly in the age of free contraception and the World Wide Webb just ask Jeeves how not to get pregnant or Google it, there is no need for this swathe of children going around killing each other. The women can bemoan and wail in the streets about lost ones and blame closed youth cubs lack of opportunities, but they knew all of this before, and still churn out their problems on an industrial scale, then point the finger at some one else for something else, when they are the core of the problem, because of the sanitised, feminised society we now live in, the question will never arise. The questioning of the females to have children is again such a taboo and contentious issue, this will never be properly discussed because it is a divine and sole right of women to have babies and how many. In that case they have sole responsibility for this act and sole responsibility to vet any suitable partners they choose to breed with. Instead all the blame is heaped upon the father, these men were never going to be present and never were present, in full knowledge of the mothers to be, past relationships, criminal registers can all be accessed on the prospective sperm donor, I very much doubt any responsibility will be exercised, after all the woman is always the "victim" and is never held financially or morally accountable.

Vile abuse erupts from the painted distorted mouth, face pinched in anger, arms flailing, claw like nails searching for their target, a man once proud and in love cowers in the corner amongst the garish yet to be paid for furniture, is this a scene from a soap opera, no, this is a reality for many men which goes unnoticed, unreported and there fore unrecorded. This is the fruits of the so called empowerment of women, fought for by ugly people, for ugly reasons, the destruction, demoralisation and absolute control over men. The systematic wish to breakdown the fathers input and social standing with in the family, to dilute the children's ideology, and how they perceive their dads, sitting half way up the stairs comforting each other, the children listen to the bullying belittlement by an unending belief, that women are better in all aspects of all aspects and if she is not, positive discrimination will prove she is.

In the dead of night, with the smell of nappies and sour milk the epiphany hits like a sledgehammer, looking down on the rough shaven, tired snoring creature beside her, lips curl into a snarl with the utterance " I'm better than this ". As we all know in the main they are not, that's why they have arrived where they now are, through their own choices, right or wrong, this was the path chosen, the wagging finger points to the man beside her, and a vow made to rectify this outrageous problem, the seed germinates in the woman's brain like a cancer of no rhyme or reason other than what ever it takes, or whatever dirty deeds that need to be employed she will overcome this oppression and life that is undervalued, the life of second rate being, just a mother raising the children is not enough, in fact it's the root cause of the problem, the man asleep unaware of the oncoming onslaught, as he is responsible for plunging her into this purgatory state, she now has to endure with no end insight. The man is now in debt to the heinous crime of love, and taking care of his family, totally unaware of the pure contempt that is held towards him by the woman he loves. At the beginning compliance is his response, due to the unexpected unfolding of all around him, inevitably the end is in sight for him, the appeasement of this selfish uncaring psychopath is grist to the mill with no end product. She now wants the independence she feels she deserves and has been denied, no more evening or weekend activities with the kids that is now her time, she comes to the conclusion, she has the kids all week, not true when the kids are at the nursery or school, the effort required to get them there is not a full time oppression they try to portray, from now on when the husband is home it's "his turn", the reasoning behind this, "it's alright for you, you have been at work all day". With six pm financially insignificant jobs and evening fridge lists, or the night school attendance where the become clever and the man becomes boring and with out ambition, she craves anything but being a mother, she can start at the bottom of the ladder of a career, low paid, subsidised by the husbands wage, a position he could never afford due the reliance on his wage to support the family.

After the fruitless forays into this and that another option is required, the ultimate game plan when all else fails, get pregnant. A half decent relationship, about 3 months, will do it. Married or not, this is the next step calculated and mercenary, she has monitored friends progress in this field, asked all the right questions and got all the right answers, it's time to employ the guilt trips, along with as many financial impediments upon the father possible until he is pummelled into submission, by her the state and the thought police (mainly women). In the event of an unplanned pregnancy, there will be only one winner, not him, not the baby, only one other left. Supported by the father, or if he wants no part of it her own father steps in, and the for ever willing state will accommodate and feed these feckless, half hearted wannabes.

The very idea of the woman stuck at home, surrounded by wet nappies and domestic drudgery is farcical take on the modern day home. With every essential appliance (and many ones not) delivered by Argos, ordered on line whilst in the usual position sat on their arse, without the need to strain a sinew to cook, clean or wash and any other task for that matter. Long gone the days of coal fires and the dust that went hand in hand with the open fire, iron framed windows with ice on the inside, coats on the bed, school clothes washed by hand and dried by the fire on Sunday evenings, beating carpets on washing lines, washing piles of dishes, oh how the modern woman should rejoice in their show houses that hardly ever get dirty, no kids playing outside, no veg to grow, no muck, only discarded prosseco tops and dairy milk wrappers down the back of the 3000 pound yet to paid for settee. With almost all day and every day to do as they wish stay at home mums have to much time on their minds, with out the sense to utilise this super opportunity of precious free time, they choose to turn this into something much more sinister.

Confiding to her peers she feels depressed and undervalued, invisible in society, isolated from friends, who have no children and are sick of hearing about hers. I find this baffling, as to how this manifests, yes I am a man and I don't understand, with all that freedom they cannot structure a situation to suit them, it's only a baby a natural occurrence, she should be able to second guess the child and control it with great efficiency, that's what she is supposed to do, yet she caves into the child, the child senses this from a very early age and the damage is done. Then the man arrives home, the woman with outstretched arms containing the baby, "it's your turn, I have had it all day", with ignorance beyond belief, to the fact that the husband has full financial responsibility for the family's survival, the need to fulfil his requirement, in a position of employment he may detest or be under severe pressure in order to balance the domestic books, and solely on his endeavours alone the family sinks or swims. This greeting is unjustified and with no thought or respect to anything other than self-serving desire, which by the way women are a ver good at.

In the event of unemployment and the money dries up, so does the cunt, everything that goes wrong is his fault, never the thought that if all bad is down to him, so therefore all the good times were exclusively of his making, that rationale will never be explored, the mother in law " I told you he was no good " the once alpha male slaughtered by financial embarrassment, she the victim, never the finger pointed at the woman who's flicking of the Argos catalogue was a sound of dread when trying to get to sleep. Does all this bring anyone with a scintilla of intelligence to the conclusion that this is an equal division of labour, other than in minds of twisted minds of the feminist influenced state. The man will end up tired, burnt out, devoid of ideas and exhausted of trying to do the write thing for everyone else, apart from him, and in many cases tossed on the scrap heap, homeless, physically ill, mentally ill, and finally the state has it's wish, another "broken man".

The Children and Family Court Advisory and Support Service

(CAFCASS) are as the length of the name suggests, a group of unqualified, overpaid windbags of which the government holds any power over. With an army of busybodies of which should surprise no one are 83% women, dining out mainly on allegations as opposed to proven evidence, of which will be skewered in the woman's favour in some tribal morass that they seem to excel at. How in any way, any one, could deem this as, a normal institution, with out bias, is frankly under-prepared for any dealings in our children's welfare or future. If you do not understand this or do not want to understand this, then you are party to the abuse of fathers and children in an unstoppable locomotive of misguided ardour, on the basis of rule of thumb, men are bad women are good. In any study of the last thirty years, they all come to the same conclusion, that the dramatic effect of all this inclusion of fake social sciences and experiments upon young boys is horrifying. With the proclivity to exclude fathers from debate and decision with the overwhelming bias by the overwhelmingly numbers of women pulling the strings, is creating everything they say are trying to avoid, fatherless families on the increase. This in turn, which is well documented, a fatherless child has more chance of the dangers of substance abuse, alcohol abuse and failings at school, and taking up criminal activities, these are just the tip of the ice berg of a fatherless upbringing of young boys. If this not enough to start a serious debate, and a complete overhaul of this particularly toxic body of people, to save the minds and souls of sons and fathers to be, in this destructive and divisive way society is being run by the likes of CAFCASS. At the moment in the seventy most developed countries boys are falling behind in education, they are sinking deeper in a world that they feel there is no part for them, this can only be an out come which will be detrimental to all.

CHAPTER NINE

oney is of course a huge factor as to who is with who, the unerring evidence here is the wives of very rich and powerful men, the obvious theme being the more money you have the more attractive the wife appears. Take Henry the viii had many such ladies, not bad for an obese man with the aroma of rotten legs, Bernie Eccelstone's statuesque wife, if Bernie was merely a tyre fitter say, would the relationship have developed. Then the pathetic notion that success is the draw, the aphrodisiac is success not money, if this is so why in divorce is the money of such importance. Let me simplify this already simple set of circumstances, the more money you have the better car you drive, the more money you have the finer the food and venue you eat it at, the woman wants to be seen at all the right places and seen driving the car that reflects her status and where she belongs in society. That's fine, if the understanding was as clearly understood by those who should know better, that the sole attainment to all these benefits relied solely on to whom these women married, not a nail bar topic I am sure.

The acquirement of wealth by deception and sexual entrapment are a very key component to the success of the marriage for money venture. Joint bank accounts, never jointly filled, the stupidity of the man in the heroic gesture of offering a stranger the keys to his wealth is astounding, the naivety of mind that thinks this is ok is a phenomenon, incomprehensible in any normal walk of life. " if you don't love me enough, or trust me enough" is the lame empty rhetoric espoused, and the men who have been corralled by women all their lives fall for it.

The fear the woman will put her prized asset into another man's hands is all it takes, some men end up in a frenzy of financial suicide and some times much worse, actual physical suicide, this sexual black mail is a tool used without any fear of accountability of the end result. This man now trapped in a scene of capitulation, not only financial, which is in it's self the biggest lever to comply to her rules. From once running his own affairs, now he can't even book a doctors appointment, she does it, and even attends with him, butting in like a drunk with heatstroke about anything from his bowels to an in growing toenail, this form of interference is the quest of control to maximise domination.

He now has no knowledge or understanding of the running of the house, usually his house, or the house they supposedly buy "together", usually a larger deposit from him, "well you earn more" she twitters. If the deposit is equal, her's usually comes with the help of a male family member, with a genuine thought that they, are helping, this "helping" is just prolonging the inadequacies of the woman in the financial side of relationships, no matter how she obtains the money, or in the event of a smaller percent being contributed by her the out come, if the relationship fails the spoils start at 50/50, this is unfair because in many cases it never starts like that. The man becomes estranged from the day to day running of the house, no interest in utility bills, special offers at Tescos and the like, she again becomes the master of the house, running all lives that reside in her domain, with neatly written rosters pinned to the fridge door, with a magnet from the shit holiday in Turkey, the last one he will be allowed to book, because he was responsible for the bad hotel, he cooked all the bad food, that gave mum the squittals (plus side she lost 9 pounds in a week, a feat never replicated, only in the opposite direction) and he is the one who ordered the turbulence on the way home, and he lost the suitcase with all her tat and fags inside. The full circle has been achieved with the stealth not yet possessed by MI5 or the KGB combined, the man has been transported back to his youth at home with his parents, told where and when he can go out, and if he oversteps the allowed circumstances, the old days of Flo waiting for Any Capp, behind the door with a rolling pin are long gone, for two reasons, one she has probably never held or even owned a rolling pin, number two as we all know, domestic violence by a woman doesn't exist. A deadlier form of abuse is in play from her, one no one can see or prove "the silent treatment" mental abuse, " the lights are on, but no one's home", unless there is an offer at Argos to good to miss, " picture and no sound " is only resumed when a girls night out is looming, when you are required as a baby-sitter for your own children. Then there is the constant home improvements, bathroom and kitchen upgrades she craves, the deadly remortgage or even worse the mortgage terms extended by ten years, she will not loose a wink of sleep over these financial matters, if only it was the same for him. Finances within a relationship are a catalyst for disaster, the spending patterns of men and women are ugly different, the woman prior to the cohabitation has been financed to some degree by male family members, this trait is then expected to continue with the boyfriend, and she has the notion she should be looked after and any shortfalls in finances be absorbed by him. Women earn less in general due to less risk taking, and the man will enter a market with higher expectation and more knowledge needed, an environment of physical and dangerous occupations, thus better paid. Normally the man earns more, this is not by luck, so on living together he is expected to shoulder any unforeseen financial burdens, the women in general have no career ambitions (only false ones) and once the exquisite taste of "part-time" has been encountered there's no going back from here, akin to the flavour of a large donor kebab that will be guarded as it devoured to the death.

So he stumps up for her birthday meal, and also his own alongside any other lame event on the calendar, also he pays for most necessities with most unnecessaries or else the shutters will come down, and life will become rather unpleasant. The paying off of the maxed out credit card rarely falls on the continuously broadening shoulders of the inept female, to extinguish the debt of the "magical money tree card", which has been used to buy the unneeded and unused and in another time would be out of reach, but the squanderlust ritual of overspending continues, until a brief unscheduled sexual encounter occurs (there is no such thing as a free blow job), then in floods of tears she spews out her regret and the " I won't do it again", my arse she won't. This sad irresponsibility and assumption someone will pick up the bill is devious, calculating and always deflected away from the perpetrator, and shows how easy it is to spend someone else's money.

She crows on about financial independence, and hates the idea of having to justify what she is spending his money on, which is one of the main topics for marital unrest, she says it's degrading to have to ask for money, (when did spending some one else's money become a problem) the need for her to earn a little money is imperative to the argument "i work too" so the spending can be justified without question.

In the event of any change in circumstances concerning relationships, the woman is always the one who is first to be recognised, in a time when the social structure is interrupted, alongside skewered legal systems the woman has just one thing on her mind, where is the free money going to come from. For instance, child maintenance, how's "he" going to pay if "he" is not working or if "he" is working how much can we screw "him" for, notice it is always "he", as woman hardly ever pay child maintenance. All the stops are pulled out for these poor women to save them from any impending hardship that may come hurtling towards them. The men are once again at the back of the queue and seen as the ones who can look after themselves, who can pay the child support, the mortgage on the house they are not even aloud in, never mind live in, and any other monies he was beaten up by the courts to sign up to. So the scant disregard for the man's needs is again trampled into the ground, with out care or redress, in the cold black sea of helplessness the sad reality is the only way out is suicide, which among young men is not surprisingly one of the main causes of death, this pummelling of innocent sole by greedy woman backed by the state must end.

When women are asked to pay child support both the state and they scoff at the very idea, in a previous study in the USA 85% of all child support came from men, and of the remainder women who did pay paid less. It is in seething contempt women have towards the once love of their lives, their soulmates, their best friends is inexhaustible, they say "you are not much of a man, if you cannot look after the kids, and need a woman's help", in this very tired argument it shows the complete inability to understand fairness and equality by these woman. In this dichotomy the state will nearly always back the woman, even the act of not pursuing her non payment of child support with the vigour the man would receive.

It's getting pretty hostile out there, and I find it a little strange that equal pay is what was fought for and won, that when it comes the time for equal payout of monies it leaves a bad taste in the mouth of these want it all for fuck all maids of honour. Whilst most men go about the paying with the attitude of that's what I expected, due to the female uprising being such a marvellous success and the financial power bestowed upon them just or not, the only reason I can see for their proclivity not to pay their way is due to men still picking up the bill and the state reluctant to change archaic laws.

In divorce one of the most ridiculous rulings that, no matter if she was picked up off the streets, with no future, never mind any belongings or finance, and she was then lavished with gifts, holidays and cars, the list goes on, that some how if the marriage breaks down she should live a life she has become accustomed to, and guess who's paying, again. This is not only the abuse of the man and what he has worked for, it is unjust and of course backed fully by the state. There is a notion with in the female twisted train of thought, that if a woman pays for a man in any thing then this is a form of empowerment, when as a man I can tell you with absolute honesty, that when I paid for a meal or holiday or bought a pair of shoes for my daughter, of which I paid for all at all times, empowerment seems a dirty and disingenuous label to put on it. Why do these women need to dress up everything they do as so vital, its been the norm for men to pay since any one cares to remember, and by the way still is. Double standards is phrase that springs to mind, when will women be expected to foot the bill, even when sometimes there is no direct benefit to them, there still is a social stigma of a man letting a woman pay the bill, this false sense of embarrassment has been employed for decades, but I am sure us men will get used to, but I am not sure the women ever will.

There are many men committing frauds and much worse to keep up a certain lifestyle for her in doors, she has no care or worry where the money comes from, as long as it keeps coming, the holidays and the champagne are enjoyed with the knowledge it is all funded by monies not completely legitimate. Inevitably the cuffs go on, her in the back ground screaming, swearing and insisting the police have the wrong man, when in her heart she is fully aware of the circumstances.

Then the day of judgement, she dressed up and face painted, listens silently when the custodial sentence is passed, she then gasps and swoons and pretends to weep uncontrollably, yet the whole drama is fully in her control, other women gather around her to administer their support to this poor helpless woman. The stool pigeon who is now facing jail time looks on, his mind numb with his own fate, when the drama abates a declaration of celibacy is announced, "i will wait for you" she cries, with one eye on the young barrister. In any other case the woman would be jailed for aiding and abetting the sharing "ill gotten gains" would be the call, enjoying benefits at some one else's loss, but of course there is no question to answer or responsibility to bare, purely due to gender, if for arguments sake, the spoils would have been shared with his best mate would the out come be the same, I think not.

The headline Britons Billionaires caught my attention, because of the inclusion of so many women, have a little knowledge of how women accrue wealth I thought I must delve into this headline a little further, due to my lack of respect to those claiming false powers of wealth creation. Of the 15 women having overwhelmed the columnist and got his juices flowing, number one was on the list purely through inheritance, no effort required, and also investment it says, it's easy to risk money you never earned never mind worked for. Number two, inheritance, a theme developing here, money passed down by successful men, if you buy the sausage meat and supply the machine and the recipe, I will put the skins on syndrome, bankrolled by fathers and grandfathers ingenuity who were generous beyond fault. Also they include the family name and history which it is clear for all to see, these women married into the money. The claim that it is surprising how many women on the list is ridiculous, more male billionaires more female ones, to claim billionaire status on ones acumen is wrong these women preside over a pile of money they had in no way had any input in accumulating. Without help or the fortunate circumstances of being born in the right, this picture of female wealth would be a lot less wholesome than the one they are so desperate to project.

The richest men however show drive and enthusiasm to make money and build successful empires on their own talents, with forward thinking, dedication and hours upon hours, week after week, year after year, and taking physical and mental risk with the stamina required. Can this be said of the aforementioned, categorically not. These men were pioneers, in invention, invention of machines, to mine diamonds and draw oil from out of the ground to mention just two, a whole library of successful male pioneers could be filled times over, that of female of the same stature would fit comfortably in a shoe box. These men did not marry into or rely on someone being put in in the ground so they could pursue stellar careers, some of these men were born in council houses and public houses, in poverty, these men rose up on the risk and endeavour, the theme being they were self made men. Women are in general mere bystanders in the business world, wheeled out at high-brow functions and endless charity balls, with the adulation of half wits sucked up akin to the latest Dyson hoover. With the tired old adage "behind every great man is a great woman", what does that mean exactly, there is a woman skulking about in the shadows waiting for his demise to step out and proclaim "it was all my idea", this notion is about as believable as a grainy night time photo of a UFO, this old girl power is misleading and nauseating to the point of idiotic folly. Why do we need to proclaim them as a successful business women, when clearly they are not, it is again an elevation of genderised fairy tales we see and endure in our daily lives, "the sisters are doing it for themselves" my bollocks they are.

CHAPTER TEN

On embarking on some ridiculous course at "uni" (how to make hand made condoms for Armadillos, maybe) this can take between 3 to 5 years of at most 15 hours a week in lectures and probably 15 minutes of research, if they see the course through. Once it dawns upon these female saviours of humanity how meaningless and worthless this chosen path is they drop out in droves, and as usual the bill goes to dad or the state. This fictitious notion they will make a difference in the world never mind a living is laughable, and a more sensible approach should be made and more sensible courses, such as Domestic Science.

With endless free courses (a working man would have to pay hundreds of pounds for this opportunity) at night school, with mantra of retraining mums to get back to work, millions of pounds spent on unfinished courses, the high light being the fag break, and of course leaving the child at home with the already tired man trying to grab a few hours of relaxation, before sleep and another early start. On attending one of these night school classes, the subject was Sociology, which I passed, the class consisted of me and eight others, all women, who were looking for careers as social workers, putting these women in charge of children in difficult circumstances was to say the least frightening. The reason being their complete lack of understanding and conception of every day life, on being cosseted and shielded all their lives by males, the grasping of a taxing set of circumstances involving violence or sexual matters seemed beyond their ability to react intuitively and give a response with out referring to the manual, which was hugely outdated and in my opinion misinformed. The whole class was soaked in well meaning to the detriment of everything they were meant to be taking on board, the total lack of knowledge of the problems they seemed confident they could overcome was an absolute sham, the travesty of failure of these women to help desperate children and the salaries they will command on becoming Social workers, is nothing short of scandalous, and they will look you in the with utter disdain having to be questioned by one such as me. On filling out a questionnaire 5 out of 8 denied to ever having driven without a seat belt, and 4 to have never broken the speed limit, this control of all they see and all they do is spellbindingly narcissistic and unhelpful to everyone. This wearing of ones arsehole for a hat rolls out across the board these over paid busy body know it all paragons who are willing to take any course (apart from un-beneficial intercourse) to put a few meaningless letters at the end of their double barrelled names. I would suggest the letters NEITS, No Experience In This Subject. With a large amount of research needed and homework required for the above mentioned night school class, whilst working full time, was a bit of a struggle, and again stay at home mums in the class, and part timers, which was most of the class, which whilst being at home all day, with or with out the kids, thus affording them the advantage of time which would give them a huge chance of passing with flying colours (a common theme through out female life, time to educate themselves, while the man is to busy working, to engage in this pursuit) this disproportionate freedom of time is always denied, this un-reported and closely guarded data would show the disadvantaged mens chance to re-train and re-educate.

Also the fact of being able to join a workplace at the bottom of the ladder, on a low salary, propped up, and indeed subsidised by the man, further more, the meeting of new people, and type of work undertaken (mostly office work, hardly ever anything manual) gives them a feeling of superiority, and unlike the man, they have bettered themselves. Through their own determination and abilities, well actually no, most cases rely on the man's financial support, the man looking after the kids (unpaid work I think she would call it), during the woman's odyssey to catapult herself into the world of high finance, or the office at the local Kwik-Fit, the delusions of grandeur abound, and the joint account bypassed. The disposing of men's ambitions on mass, through unfair championing of women's right to further education, with back door sexism again shows the diminishing life chances men are now experiencing, and systematically being put at the back of the queue, in a society so driven by the discrimination of men, it has lost sight of the balance it set out to address. This blind attrition will be continued to the point of the man's well being all but overlooked by overweight, over subsidised, over zealous group of people prioritised by gender, above anything else.

Mathematics is the latest chasm to be crossed for our poor little female students, and as to why they do not get involved enough, if a female does not sign up A level maths it tells me (little old me) two things, it is either to difficult for them or they are more interested in less taxing subjects, which in a round about way, says they are not up to it. The boys, obviously have more aptitude for mathematics, but how can that be, next thing, we cannot allow that to be. The state must not allow it to be, after much gnashing of teeth, and head scratching, until blood oozes out, we must bring the boys down to the girls level. Penalise the boys until the girls catch up. It is the state duty ?, to rectify this travesty in an education system that is rotten to the core, with the ideology that if you are good at some thing, and being male, you must be undermined and confidence eroded, until the girls are on par, surreptitious obstacles must be implemented until the balance is redressed in the girls favour so we can over come this gross miscarriage of justice. In the states constant meddling run by fifth rate jobs worths, left wing think tanks filled with dunderheads, the state introduced the all singing all dancing HE's Athena SWAN charter, what the fuck is that I hear you cry, after removing your jaw from whatever flooring you may be standing on. The full title is advance Higher Educations Athena Scientific Woman's Academic Network charter. The Athena being, a wonderful old war horse Athena Donald, a highly esteemed academic who on behalf of those unwilling or unable or both being included in all subjects which whistle quietly over female heads. Since its official launch on the 22/09/2005 to address the "problem" of gender numbers not to her liking in Science, Technology, Engineering, Medicine and Mathematics (STEMM) and in may 2015 also included Arts, Humanities, Social Sciences Business and Law disciplines. This mind-boggling miasma can only lead to an unfair advantage to skew the education system to favour girls, this is nothing short of criminal abuse of power, backed totally by the state. This just goes to show no stone no matter how big or small will go unturned achieve the results the state feels is correct and just. After a some what lengthy 14 years of it's SWANN being introduced, mathematic professors consist of 94% men, 6% women, how much more time and money has to be wasted in trying to fit square pegs into round holes, to please those few so called elite academics, who are trying to make girls do some thing they have no interest or aptitude, to socially engineer in the foulest manner to make things look how they feel they must look, these deranged and power-hungry and very dangerous people should be seen for what they are, as the above statistic shows, failures. If all was revealed in any other walk of life, derision would be constant, but as in all Politically Correct endeavours the hat has to be pulled down like a drunk cowboy in front of a crackling camp fire, after a long day in the saddle with out a thought for tomorrow.

So what exactly is the predicament, and what are the reasons for the predicament, secretly we all know there is no predicament, girls are for some reason not as good at maths as boys, for the same reason some can sing and some cannot, yes, training can be given, but this will never substitute natural talent and ability, why do these manipulative and divisive left wing academics.

When these square pegs have been hammered through round holes, the shape will become distorted and also the hole, the result is the once recognisable shape is now unnatural shape, a deformed shape, how in any ones mind is this programme allowed to continue or even be championed as a worthy cause. One train of thought is that girls feel intimidated in mathematics, my thought is there is only one answer to the sum, not a proliferation of ways to dislodge the out come as in say sociology, so if the sum is wrong there is no manoeuvre for reasoning against the out come, one of the traits women will rely on through out their lives. I am told mathematics is tiered, so if you miss a year the level is lost, of course maternity will at some point force the interruption of studies, but this is a tired issue reeled out at as an excuse as to why women are failing at almost anything in life.

CHAPTER ELEVEN

Domestic abuse is another issue conveniently statistically massaged into a thunderous orgasm, for the benefit of women by certain pressure groups, who need to be dragged into the real world and not just the world they dominate and inhabit. I am referring to the lack of acknowledgement that female on male abuse ever happens. Mat Hancock a leading figure in the conservative party on discussing the 2020 corona virus pandemic said due to the isolation of family households, "Women and children in a domestic abuse situation, will not be forgotten ". In condemning men to non-existence and silence again, shows why men are systematically over-looked and under funded in the cases of domestic abuse perpetrated against them by women, in which they are one third of all victims. That is why the statement " over-whelming majority" (of victims are women) narrative has been successfully challenged in court, and is no longer a lawful mantra feminists can dine out on.

Domestic abuse on men has dramatically increased since 2009, in which 27000 cases of men reported abuse, to 92000 in 2018, taking into account that a significant number of men will never admit to abuse for reasons of embarrassment or just feeling they won't be believed, to name just two, (this is certainly not the case for women) or the figures would be even higher. As for the availability of refuge hostels this is solely for women, for many males, one of the cynical levers used by women to eject the male from the family home is the accusation of domestic abuse, the man, unfortunately ends up on the street. As for the women, enjoying the comforts of home, and all the obsequious attention they can stomach, which by the way is a fair bit, are 60 % more likely to be the abusers themselves, gerrymandering of genders always in plain sight of anyone who takes an interest, unfortunately that does not include the state. The unwillingness by the state to recognise, let alone deal with the problem, and it's tragic consequences, is another example of the women before men approach which exists in many guises, in the name of equality in all things, apart from the things which do not directly benefit women or the things they are not keen on, bricklaying and walking the dog on dark winter mornings to mention just two.

Parental alienation is another form of abuse, cruelly employed in the main by women, excuses for the denial of the basic right to see ones children, this can be financial or court order not adhered to (how about punitive measures in line with the non-payment of maintenance, of course this is a non-runner, because the overwhelming payers of maintenance are men). Coercive control with in relationships is made out to be again a purely male trait, with claims dating back to Victorian times and some to cave men, or should I say cave people eras, these wild and astonishing acts in a bygone era, are somehow deemed to be happening in the present, in the "that happened to me" by the monotoned, mawkish and and miserable desperadoes, to justify their self appointed non-existence. One of the methods employed is said to be depravation of food, unless you living in a house together and are never more than one metre apart, 24 hours a day, how can this enforced diet be implemented. How could this condition be maintained, if the husband is at work, does he count the slices of bread and the frozen peas before he leaves the house, then in return check her teeth for any sign of food consumption (freshly brushed teeth are a certain red flag) all of this sounds ridiculous, but so is the idea that a competent adult human being, could not have a cunning way to divert the odd packet of fig rolls or maybe Pringles into ones mouth. On looking at most married women the depravation of food, is the last thing they are experiencing, in their traumatic troubled lives.

Another method is said to be isolation from family and friends, with my vast experience in these matters, the woman is far more likely to engage in this, and with more success, with their bitchy and jealous characters. How many brothers do you know who are not on speaking terms, compared to sisters who are at constant loggerheads, with one-upmanship or should I say one-upwomanship, jealous of furniture and white goods, many brothers would funnily enough, not be to concerned about contact with sisters. Friends are a different dynamic, when kids come along it is a normal thing that free time is less for both, or is it ?, he is at work, whilst in the main she remains at home, in many cases swigging wine and playing councillor to the next door neighbour, who gladly reciprocates the act, all of this divisive vomit spewed out in the back ground, day-time television concurs. This can only cause a rift in any relationship, a slight chagrin would be felt, even by the modest and the meek. Real friends are never a bother in any situation, but the modern day collusion between women fully backed by the state at all times, is enough to make most men dubious of the outcome.

Money is another form of coercive control we are told, is it true the online clothes retailers have been thwarted at all costs, accounts closed down, all of this to avoid the constant visits by white van man, pulling up outside, filled to the gunnels with pointless and unnecessary garments, that have been browsed online hour after hour. The squandering of money on 3 year old settees, 5 grand a pop, new curtains (who ever notices curtains), kitchens tacked onto an already over baring mortgage, all for what, just to keep up with the Joanses, can any one who has not been certified recently describe this as financial cruelty, the only cruelty involved is the expectations of women of the men toiling endless hours, to enable this obscene behaviour. So what is financial abuse, after house keeping paid, bills paid, what of surplus money, if any, is it put in a joint account, is that an account where all the bills come out of (not usually), both have a card for the account ?, then who decides what on and how much to spend. In my experience it's easier to spend someone else's money, if you do not value how it was obtained, as by an outdated law with in the marriage all is equal, apart from the need to take hard physical dirty jobs to balance the household books, all assets no matter how or who made them (usually the man) must be 50/50, there are to many women using the husband's salaries as a money-pit, a top up of there inability to earn more than they spend, can you blame any man who tries to ensure less is spent than what is coming in, and this is where the marital arguments arise, not out of financial abuse, but out of financial nous, of which is rarely found in women. There is another dynamic at play here, she knows if she cleans him out, and squanders all, there is always another fool to take the baton, be it the state or another deluded man, he has no such comfort blanket to suck on. He is acutely aware in the event of separation 95% of the time he will end up homeless, she will be wrapped in cotton wool by all those around her, he will by vilified as matter of fact, her bills will be paid by the state, and to add insult to injury the state will confiscate as much money out of his future earnings to give to her, to plough on with this financial immaturity that led to this sad sorry state of affairs. She and others will be oblivious to any wrong doing on her part, but throughout her life this type of conduct will be the norm.

In 2017 it is documented that 97% of complaints of coercive behaviour in Liverpool came from women, this goes to show how willing women are to accuse without proof at will, to any thing she sees or hears that she does not agree with. As with all this overload of modern day duties, think tanks and sociological masturbating the women believe nothing is their fault and want to hold men responsible for their irresponsibility and failings, whether it involves inadequacies, in friendship, financial astuteness, or what they eat or when they sleep, it's absurd to suggest men can control an adult human being in modern day England, the numbers said to be in this situation is even less likely.

In days gone by the horrible term "henpecked" was all around, in all classes, always seen as somewhat amusing and harmless, almost an endearment, a great English tradition. Many sit- coms found this form of mental abuse grist to the mill, in Keeping Up Appearances the abuse was relentless, Richard (the husband) constantly belittled by Hyacinth (the wife), was absolutely cringeworthy and hard to watch at times, this poor example of a down trodden husband was the core of amusement in not only sit-coms but the females favourite the Soap Opera. These double standards are always made out to be unimportant, just a bit of fun, Last of the Summer Wine was another sit-com set in a Yorkshire village, three retired men frequented visited the local cafe, made to look like children as the buxom old lady owner barked instructions, alongside Nora Batty was always at hand to join in the derision of these men, usually culminating in the act of herding them out the cafe with a broom, in the back ground the canned laughter resonated. Is this not a form of coercive behaviour, should it be a source of amusement, laughed at by millions, winning television awards, imagine switching the female characters to males and visa versa, I feel theses sitcoms would soon have been shelved, if ever made at all. The strange thing is, they are still shown in these modern times of oversensitivity, why when the likes of Love Thy Neighbour was banned many a moon ago for unacceptable racist content, are these sexist programmes still aired.

During the course of the menstruation cycle the female's behaviour seems to skyrocket out of control without the merest hint of a challenge as to why, the chemical imbalance of the brain is said to be the overriding cause, what imbalance is this, is it due to the fall of hormones which are a chemical substance that enters the blood from the Endocrine gland, to effect certain parts of the body, if there is a fall in hormonal output, then why the scatty behaviour, as less hormone less effect on what ever part of the body, so the lack of hormone also makes the women rude and utter immoral cruel things to husband and children. The production of Oocytes is managed by Oestrogen and Progesterone, both hormones enhance the chances of wanting and actually becoming pregnant. If these natural occurrences are to prepare the body for the wonderful event of childbirth, how can they be aligned with the nasty belligerent and down right aggressive behaviour directed at men. In the event of a woman to woman (same sex) marriage would the behaviour be the same, or would the trend be debunked, due to both parties awareness of this flawed and unnecessary situation that millions of men endure every month of every year. When the drop in hormones occurs apparently, mood swings are induced, but not in all women. This tells me that the Menstrual Cycle is used as another tool (for the exclusive use of women) to justify the way women choose to act, and again empower women to to behave with impunity.

Whilst living with a woman eggshells were very carefully traversed at this "time of the month", after being berated for the most innocuous thing, the phone rang, she answered with a calm and pleasant manner, on questioning the change in her manner, she exclaimed, "because you are here". Now this exposes the myth that mood swings cannot be controlled, and are unavoidable . This is a form of bullying to take one's anger out on an innocent party and can only be described as such. Another major issue is that the daughters will replicate this unnecessary behaviour, affecting their future relationships, and with out this behaviour being took to task and discussed it will continue. With the improvements of sanitary products, the female abilities have gone through the roof, endless adverts of women riding cycles and performing perfect cartwheels to show there are no leaks, all this claim of woman there still is an element of taboo regarding menstruation, I feel the only taboo is the question of female behaviour during this natural cycle. If you had an office of twenty women in various stages of the menstrual cycle how could it function, within this mire of uncontrolled individuals, the truth is they can control this misbehaviour as any other form of misbehaviour by man or woman, it is the choice which is lacking.

Its in part the woman's art of willing to please and at the same time deceive, carried out in such a subtle manner, it goes undetected for years. The coffee table magazines, the bible to women all across the land who wish to aspire beyond the four walls they are cruelly trapped in, domestic drudgery and oppression, rearing a child, combined with the vastly underestimated difficulty of housework, of which with the loss of most of our dirty heavy industries almost entirely the man's preserve, the filth he had to endure being brought home all but gone. With the invention of all the wonderful house hold appliances, all invented by men, we are still led to believe that the house work is a war of attrition, until of course the inevitable happens, the man takes over, then the level of difficulty will be down graded.

Even in the event of a celebratory meal coercion is at play, the expectation of the man to pay, the act of "going Dutch", not sure how this saying came about, maybe women in Holland are a little less financially demanding compared to the English women. On my observation whilst my self involved in a one way pay meal, I watched as the happy young couple entered the restaurant, excited and playful and tactile, they look around at the lavish surroundings, she in adoration, he in trepidation. They share each others food and gaze into cloudy love filled eyes, hardly a word spoken, and the meal is over in what feels like seconds. Then the bill arrives, a brief chat, and the mist descends, her once cloudy eyes narrow to slits, as she examines each and every charge, in different circumstance no item would have been questioned (him paying all) she dutifully pays her half, with a difficult smile to the waiter, they get up to leave, no eye contact, and the gap widens between them as they head for the door. This type of female exception of men to finance all and sundry, which is of course vehemently denied, with a "i pay my way", sorry love no you do not, just look at the pile of receipts skewered on the bar of any restaurant, and I am confident that where the meal was enjoyed by man and woman, his card details will be on the receipt.

I am pretty sure that the reason men remarry is the fear of being alone, they take over poisoned chalices, as they are made to feel being single is not the way society should be, so they feel compelled to remarry in a misguided belief it will give them a stake in society, a feeling not to be left out, that life will pass them by without a partner to stroke, a soulmate to steer them through the morass called life. Well let me tell these men, these empty carcasses of self pity, the forfeiting of ones dignity to an overweight baggage laden wanna be is not the answer. Boredom will again set in, deja-vu returns with vengeance, Saturday food shopping, television differences, the realisation in bed, which is one of the main reasons we are attracted to each other, the once a week request is soon rebuffed, due to lack of interest. Slowly slipping down the pecking order, second to step children, grand kids and the dog, becoming the second class citizen they where trying to avoid, somebody in the armchair unnoticed and completely ignored, unless a lift to the hairdressers is required, or some financial emergency crops up.

CHAPTER TWELVE

The entirety of existence of most wimmin revolves around delusion and deceit, one question, why wear a dress up around your arse and try to arouse men when you have no desire for 99% of them, why do they seek to arouse the very people they despise, it's for the pursuit of gain, and a testing ground for the level of manipulation required to seduce and suppress the quarry that best suits their future needs. Yes I hear you cry a person should be allowed to wear whatever one wants, even if it is solely to attract attention, the attention of those worthy suitors, and money is as always top of the list, and shortfall in this department, even a hint of it on informal, delicate interrogation the chase is off. The acres (in some women's case, literally) of exposed flesh on show, this flaunting of beauty (not always that beautiful, comments are very unwise, as even the slightest piece of well meaning advise is taken as a verbal abuse and will end in floods of tears) has throughout history placed women upon a stage that if it was down to merit, they would never have adorned.

With make up (why do women wear make up, no body seems to know (oh yes we do) it's expected, it's for self confidence the list goes on) plastered on top of fake tan on top of foundation and so on until they feel adequately camouflaged to enter the public arena. White wine, vodka and oven chips round up the pre-match warm up so the ground can be hit running, and any feeling of not being up to the mark is extinguished, emboldened by chemicals worn and others imbibed, the game is on. Once this objective has been achieved, it's a taxi to the destination, (fare shared of course) the pub for drinks, individually purchased, it is extremely rare to see women buying rounds, even for friends, this buying of a single drink enables the female to look single, and maybe encourage a hapless male into relieving the financial burden in exchange for a little small talk. Then it's on to the night club, a venue in its self perfect subterfuge, very dimly lit, extra camouflage, for women to portray themselves as the very thing they are not, this combined with loud music to combat the need for any articulate conversation.

Going to bed with Madonna and waking up with Hilda Ogden is a pleasant way to describe this type of female fraud. When the men enter the clubs (if allowed in by the bouncers, trying to save as much fanny for themselves as possible) they trawl the swamp like misty dark humid surroundings with it's array of weird and wonderful beasts, to see which one is in need of refreshment, at exorbitant prices, the female may well insist on buy the first, knowing full well this will be her last purchase of the evening. At the end of the one of two will experience a new bedroom, no prizes for guessing who pays the taxi. This coming together may well end up in a meaningful relationship, usually not, after all when the box has been opened the intrigue soon evaporates. In saying the more bedrooms visited, on the law of averages, says the desired out come will be achieved, entrapment, control and at the very least access if only temporary to the man's finances, may it be free drinks, dinners and maybe a free-be holiday. Her net contribution, whatever is in her knickers. Such is the basic need of the man he fails to notice the agenda before him until it's to late, the niceness is swathed in the impenetrable cloak of love.

Then the courtship begins, this endless fascination in each others private parts will soon diminish, as she starts to employ the very asset that started it all, with cries of "it's not all about that" oh yes it is, or was, "that's not everything" oh yes it was, the pre-marriage mantras come thick and fast and strangely not heeded, in a feeling things will improve, a flaw in the males human nature. This is akin to going out for a meal, having one mouthful, and the plate being removed, and a promise of returning the plate when they feel like it, and saying "that's not what it's all about" we can still have conversation and laughter, this may well be so, but at the end of the evening the man is still hungry.

CHAPTER THIRTEEN

When the suffragettes set out on their journey of idealism, if they were to be transported to modern times, how would they love to live in a society such as ours, with it's birth control, menstrual products, and all the unearned and unfounded adoration. With a determination to first secure the vote, and equal rights, employment rights and so on, if they were to have a peek into the future, and see the over weight dumpsters, baby machines on perpetual furlough, they would turn in their graves, bustle permitting.

This idea of including all, and including the ones who have no interest to be so, is a drain on resources and completely dilutes any credibility these super human, super intelligent beings of the master race, we now know as women. The desperate need to continue in political experiments they wish to force on the mainstream public, who's day to day struggle is beyond the aforementioned agenda, were is the fight to enable more female coalminers, the argument for more jobs on deep sea trawlers, this may sound ridiculous, but it is not as ridiculous as the avoidance of such conversations. These idiots peddle there propaganda in left wing cesspits known as universities without question, fuelled on cheap booze, and even cheaper low grade cocaine, alongside rape claims and an unfinished thesis on such valuable subjects like, a three year study on the thorax of the Tibetan wasp, 15 hours a week max. How can any one take these women serious, the answer is they take each other serious, in a cocoon of self-serving adulation, they gleefully congregate and coagulate.

As with any type of awards, wether it be university graduation, A level results, or even a red carpet event, the over representation of women is a common theme throughout, considering the higher levels of academia are held mostly by men, also the movies are also predominantly watched by men, of which the lead role is usually a man. Why are we forced time and time again to swallow these lies, is it to make things better or just to make women feel better, to make the non aspirators feel in some way included and involved and vital in all things. As for the red carpet women wear as little as possible, at the same time professing an interest in women's welfare and fight against sexual abuse whilst letting it all hang out seems a little rich. The "up to me what I wear" brigade (I would prefer they wore nothing) seem fixed on exploiting there own flesh to compensate the lack of acting ability, the double standards are always there, Julia Roberts selling her self for a million dollars became a female icon, but Sharon in Bradford who needs a few quid for a packet of fags and a bottle of White Lightening is a lowlife breaking the law, on the red carpet tits swinging, nails done, tooth veneers, thousand pound hair, oh how the suffragettes would be proud of there contemporaries. What is the man's nail bar, maybe, Kwik Fit get some new tyres or exhaust or both, pay for it, and take the fucking kids with you and pick up a Macdonalds on the way home, as it's my day off when it's your day off. All this bitterness is cultivated by the left, with the trilling of young women, who on the subject of life are as competent as a blind chicken in brain surgery, this constant meddling in an attempt to to destabilise the norm, into which for better or worse has mostly succeeded, this rhetoric that men press women and dominate the world, are fanning a fire they started, which will run out of oxygen, but not until all the ghosts of Dunkirk and the Somme have been recognised, by these female book burning, people pleasers who wish to disrupt all we know, and all they will never know. When these women have had their way and all the attributes of of men, once deemed not only good but necessary, have been washed away and expunged from history and any modern dialogue massaged into a place to suit this new model army of women. Will they be satisfied, i don't think so, due to the fact they are unaware of the consequences, of recklessly trampling over young boys and men, to whom most will end up married to. With this dumb belief you can force and smash society into what women want by force of law and violation of the male perspective on life is obscene, and after all the hot air women in all their guises will come to realise women need men and men need women, this will never change or stop being the bedrock for the survival of humanity.

I read once that if a martian was to observe the olympic games he would come to the conclusion that the world was run by black people, now if you watch the BBC morning television the martians would be forgiven for coming to the conclusion women ruled the world. When is this plethora of female non-entities, and self-important experts on any thing you do or do not car to mention going to end. Switching on morning television it's not long before they appear, head of this chief advisor of that, along with councillors for hedgehogs and alternative medicine for bananas. Any cause is taken up by these "nothing else better to do" wittering idiots. This runs alongside the endless female authors, columnists, world weary reporters and any other factotum find time to bleat on about. These so called professionals are mostly funded by banker or even more professional husbands (who of course vehemently deny all of this, in order to maintain the myth and avoid any confrontations) or how an earth could these women fit in three kids, cooking, cleaning and laundry, and of course learn a new language, in tandem with a degree in Siberian Reindeer handling. They do say multi-tasking is trait found solely in women.

Back in the day the Labour Party tried to overcome it's embarrassment by setting quotas for female inclusion, no matter what they had to offer. With delights such as Jack smith, Harry

Hymen and who could forget Henry Blears, these male wannabes but cannabes, tried to discredit any one who dared to disagree with their ideals. Due to their misfortune at birth, they would try endlessly to make every men feel like a misfortune. As I sit with my five year old daughter watching Bob the Builder with Wendie's extensive knowledge of all aspects of the construction industry, I cannot help but feel in many walks of life this misrepresentation of every day situations can only cause my daughter future harm and confusion. I am a construction worker of 40 years and only a hand full of Wendies have I encountered. So all you metro-sexual put away the baby wipes and stop hanging on to every word she utters as if it was an earth shattering subliminal statement. Never forget, men look after women, women look after women. This dynamic is emboldened with out question.

Now we have computer programmes to eradicate gender bias with in text, it is claimed this will enhance the employment chances of women, back door, underhand tactics in play again, to show how terribly treated and undervalued these, who we are constantly reminded are superior to men, are being discriminated by text. Irrelevant of suitability and capability, this one fits all mentality is pathetic and patronising, but the women seem ok with it. One click of a button and miraculously the text is cleansed and purified for the female jobseekers, by the change of a word or phrase the female is putt ease and feels she is up to the job, slight changes such as "creative" into "detailed thinker" is said to break down all the inequalities and woes of years gone by. It is claimed vacancies would be filled quicker with this technology in place, the enablement of women to manipulate the job market is deeply questionable. Take an advert for bricklayers, this would never be scrutinised or the need to change wording, because women do not want this hands on hard work, so the adverts for jobs they want, jobs that entail a lot of talking and little else, have to be tailored to suit women and make them feel they are the correct candidate, regardless. This type of interference in anything and everything to do with sole benefit of women is a cancer in modern society, the gerrymandering of all women feel is not to their liking, will in turn end up with women being who horned into positions they have no competence for, incurring poor performance in public services, a female favourite, as it is unaccountable and shrouded in equality laws second to none, private services and industries are a little less concerned with gender and more with competency.

Our language is being threatened in many ways, not least of all by "because we can" and fully backed by the "time for change" mob, being policed by these so called academics and social scientists is to the detriment all, the removal of boundaries to suit the erecting of new ones, can only create chaos and confusion to all, the main group in society under the biggest threat are young boys and men, exponential changes are undermining their roles in society. Day to day erosion of the male domain in the name of "the need to change", when the change they really want is on a selection of walks of life that best suits them, easy clean jobs is the desired outcome, being able to play male sports with excessive government funding, which when the winter comes will be dropped quicker than the learning of a musical instrument, the need to be included until the inclusion impinges on easy street and appliance is required and always the sticking point. Free invitations to colleges, to learn trade and engineering, that after a short period will be given up on, (hence the poor ratio of women in construction) when the dirt and muck begins to stick and the rain comes, icy winds blow on top of windmills to be abseiled on for repair, a career change may well occur, a warm office beckons, non taxing mundane clerical work, has given way to trowel and lathe, money wasted on training and equipment, boys overlooked in the name of diversity, girls installed in unsuitable courses by ill advised people in charge of things they don't understand desperate to go the extra mile in favour of girls. These don't call me darling types are riding roughshod of boys futures, restricting their life chances, to falsely enhance girls into fields they are not suited to or want. With out challenge or dialogue to address this systemic shift in power alongside the belief women have been held back, so now must be at the front, at all costs and no matter how much it costs.

The generic use of the pronoun "he" is to be banned, because it excludes women, really, does anyone really believe this with an ounce of integrity and honesty, I find it hard to comprehend what benefit this ridiculous type of change can have, the ambition of these dunderheads can only be the destruction of normality, this will entail a mishmash of all things that separate male and female characteristics. When the blurring of society is complete and anarchy is upon us, and the fight to restore a balance is needed, who will step up to curtail this snow ball of hate and indecision and patch up the whole created by these women, don't hold your bollocks or your breathe waiting an admission of any wrong doing on their part, with the self acclaim pumped into these women by the state and feeble men and the pandering of academia across the board, all in fear of saying the wrong thing, I can't believe these intelligent men hold the views they espouse, the only reason they conform to this Orwellian talkspeak is to save their well paid jobs, and image of not being a misogynist, so they dare not divert from the expected mantras.

magine a remake of Twelve Angry Men, to Twelve Slightly Annoyed Women, the original is an outstanding movie on the jury wrestling with conscience and coincidence on the life of a boy accused of murdering his father, an all male affair from start to finish. I suppose in our brave new world this movie would never have been made, due to lack of diversity and many other reasons.

The emotion and frustration and bullying is a cinematic feast, with the jury being all male, the empathy and sense of justice are played out beautifully, by a male cast who's powerful display show every one why the male actor has a stronger presence and there is more gravity to the movie due to the all male cast. Actresses (now known as actors?) could never instil this electrically charged environment of anger without tears, thus diluting the whole scenario, to an over emotional weepy weak spectacle. In a vipers nest of of thoughts and beliefs, and the diversity of the male characters which could never be found in the female spectrum is all part of the movies success and acclaim, this type of high octane performance is maintained through out, women rarely have the stamina or charisma to engage the public in this manner.

So who could we cast in the remake, Michelle Keegan, maybe, lorded once in the epic saga Coronation Street, which entails the same level of art as the screeching violins on school parents evening, could you imagine her or any other actress in the extended monologues captivating the audience in the same way as Henry Fonda, Lily Savage would be more plausible. Who would play the part of Lee J Cob, the coincidence was all he needed, sweat stained armpits, a get this done attitude, a huge presence, a large man, what actress could carry it of, maybe Rebel Wilson could have a stab at, that would be worth the entrance fee alone. The part of Edwin Bins, would maybe to Jennifer Anniston, one could just imagine her exercising the huge power of performance, saving an old man from the bullying, with cut throat devastating acting of nothing other than sheer terror and fear saturating the room. Now Joseph Sweeny, the little frail old man, maybe, Mavis of Coronation Street fame, with her "don't really know" catchphrase stunning the room into silence. This remake would enforce what is already known, men have more power of presence on screen thus there is no mystery why they are paid more. Viewers like intense drama, and action, hero's and villains, it is just not believable to imagine these women fast and ruthless roles, one cannot imagine one's mum, throwing a fourteen stone man over her shoulder, and then leaping on a speeding car's bonnet, it just looks silly.

Is it any surprise that women are not as well represented in the making of movies, directors and producers (the one's who put the money up) are by and large men, men are more creative and have a broader conception of reality, directors must be trusted by producers make a movie that that makes money, men are top of the tree in this art, thus more prolific in the industry. Women seem to have the notion that if given license to make movies, it must be highjacked for an agenda, wether it be forcing fat women into unsuitable roles, black women over represented, or the over zealous portrayal of the all conquering female, out thinking, out fighting the physically superior male, this is driven be the need to force their opinions and prejudices on any thing the feel is not going their way, all of these things contribute to some women being overlooked in the film industry. Women are even more to be in the minority in the making of factual programmes, this is the result in the lack interest in the matter, this theme is through out female attitudes on life in general, a litmus test for my argument, go to the local news agents early in the morning, men out number women hugely in the purchasing of newspapers, not difficult, the very few women who are up early, would be more likely to purchase fags or chocolate, and in some cases still in their bed clothes. The costume designers in the movies are usually women, no complaints or jealousy are manifested by men because of this statistic, the old adage "horses for courses" springs to mind, of which women always seem to be running head on into the field, instead of with it.

The term old masters in things such as paintings by Rembrandt or Vermeer, is now under threat, as in any other description including the word master, head master, master of the hunt and so on is a major concern for the gender police, even good old master Bates will have to walk the plank to satisfy these whinnying pariahs of modern day madness. The word master or magister as it is in Latin, really has no gender, it just means to be head of or in control of something. It just so happens, that men to be in control or head of most things, for whatever the reason maybe, (of many I have written about previously) is why the term master gas been genderised to suit the unsuitable. The term mistress is more commonly used to describe a lady of disrepute, so may the gender police will try to ban that too.

CHAPTER FIFTEEN

Because of the onset of the Coronavirus we are led to believe women are a the hardest hit, again the hand wringing supporters of these inadequates shows how reliant on pity they have become. Women's jobs are more at risk, well this is down to demand and need, a person making coffee for a living or a person fixing cars, a person laying and repairing utility services or a person answering the phone, with this you need to look no further than the female and male workplaces as to why women are more likely to be retained in employment or furloughed, it's the harder jobs which are in their nature more important, and it just happens to be mostly men who take them on.

Some women even requested to be furloughed to spend more more time with the kids, in doing this the realisation that it was not as hard as they have preached for the last thirty years, the applications to train as nannies has shot up tenfold, easy street beckons once more. Of course there is a more sinister side to lockdown, the women have been doing more housework than their male equals, old dogs and all that, with the rush on nursery training and the new found idleness of stay at home mums on the rise, will the fight for job quotas and equality become a thing of the past, if you can see through the propaganda, lies and the I want it alls (well not the dirty jobs, or any responsibility or accountability in the workplace, the list goes on) attitude, you will soon realise we have been sold a pup, a dead one at that. All these monolithic game changers after all want to stay at home, on realisation, it's a damn site easier than work.

Then of course the state will have to regulate and set up new departments to understand the dynamic as to why these woman have left the workforce during the pandemic and not returned, this will be of course womanned entirely of middle aged women, overpaid and underworked, with an outcome of astounding irrelevant and meaningless twaddle. There will be another tremendously important segment of society to pander to, the new breed stay at home mums, who will require government guidelines, think tanks set up of none entities on the division of labour within the household, such as who washes the dishes and who dries the dishes, this vital use of taxpayers money will supersede Brexit and the collapse of the economy, after all if these females are willing to give up highflying careers in call centres, Tesco, Oliver Adams (never in the butchers, maybe to cold) then we as a nation must afford them protection in their hour of need after the sacrifice they have yielded, all they believe in and have fought so hard for, in the last thirty years, maybe a bank holiday in honour of these meaningless careers now in tatters.

The children are getting fat due to lockdown, well, no, they were pilling on the weight way before this, due to oversized mums dishing out oversized meals, this is really simple and beyond any argument, that the less you eat the less you will weigh, and in most cases it is the mother who is in full control of consumption. The dieting industry has been around for decades and is worth millions of pounds, because it promises women they can loose weight with the littlest effort possible and still eat their favourite foods, who in their right mind would believe this, let alone pay for this nonsense, the desperate, that's who. These we are told are educated women, taking up these diets, who think with virtually no exercise and the continuation of their diet the pounds will simply fall off because some diet plan says so, these plans have been rejigged and regurgitated to suit each generation to whom it may concern, with little or no evidence they actually work.

Women are now becoming the chief holders of allotments (as long as the old man digs it I presume) due to the lockdown, we are led to believe they are turning in their droves to grow their own as it were. Could all this unseasonably good weather have a part to play in this, all this tottering around in Hunter green wellies has been quite a wheeze I dare say, until it is time to get back to work, will they find time in the evenings to water and weed as their dedicated male counterparts do so diligently, I fear not, after being inspired by Barbara in The Good Life, I would hazard a guess that more of the Margo will come into play. When it's time to put a new roof on the shed or some guttering is in need of repair, so water can be skilfully diverted into the newly installed water butt, they will be again be found wanting in a man's world, these hands on tasks seem to be all but out of the female's reach. When the nights draw in and the temperature drops the rain will fall, and the boots become heavy with mud, and the hands are chapped and grubby, how many of these eager little beavers will you see at dusk in the week after work, or at eight am on a cold wintery morning. The numbers will rapidly subside, not unlike the Christmas gift gym memberships in February, anything that requires effort or dedication is again swerved by most women, who pursuit is usually the less taxing kind, Coronation Street and on line bingo to name but two much preferred pastime in the event of inclement weather.

The pandemic has "no respect for the patriarchy' according to Sonia Sodha, a so called news reporter, I find this deeply insulting when it is more white males of the UK who are dying, it is as usual in any circumstances the weapon of hate has to be brandished by these very sad and boring individuals. Many women claim they have lost their job because of the pandemic have just simply quit, that is not loosing your job, it is giving it away, as with the grinding despair which women claim they are the only victims is like my hair, wearing a little thin, like the badly played piano the plink plonk has gone on far to long.

It is the nature of women's work, that's was it has been impacted more, being as we are promised more pandemics, maybe the women will take up more demanding jobs, dirty jobs, dangerous jobs, skilled jobs, just to cover another eventuality, no, that's just not going to happen, they whine about the lost 3 hours a day in the cafe (keep it under sixteen hours a week or the benefits might be stopped) or the part time job shared at the local council office, many of these unnecessary jobs, of course will go when the belt is tightened. They say men are showing no compassion for the female plight, does it not occur to these women that men might just have had enough of all this, demands to be treated equal in all things, other than the ones they don't want to be equal in, and then expect to be cosseted by men who in many cases are facing uncertainty of their own.

Also with the schools being closed due to the virus, the idea that hard science would be given preference at the cost to humanities, makes absolute sense to put first the most important and useful subjects first, but the spanner in the works is again women, they claim it to be unfair to ask them to take up subjects they are not good at, the wishy washy humanities with the cover of ambiguity in every answer is more to their liking, as nearly always the women prefer the easy option, that's fine no one cares, just stop whittling on that every thing is against your chance of being a success, when the only person who can make you a success is you.

www.ingramcontent.com/pod-product-compliance
Lightning Source LLC
Chambersburg PA
CBHW050920260726
48660CB00001B/304